But Something Is There

Not your Father's Close Encounter

BY STEVE NEILL

Chief Editor: Mary Cacciapaglia
Photography by Steve Neill
Illustrations by Paul Butcher

But Something is There
Copyright © 2017by Steve Neill

ISBN**978-1973911210**

Dedication

This book is dedicated with love to

My beloved Father, Thomas J. Neill
 Who gave me much affection and my first telescope ~ Dad was lost when to me when I was 13
years old

My Grandfather Neill with whom I loved and shared
the unknown

My step-grandfather, Philip Carnahan who taught
me about the stars

You all live in my heart and I'm grateful for everyday
your light shines on me still.

Forward

I have known Steve Neill since I began my Hypno-therapy practice and Alien Abduction research work 25 years ago.

Like so many who seek me out for regression therapy in an attempt to uncover strange and unnerving memories from as far back as they can recall, Steve seemed nervous and a bit apprehensive. However, his need to finally know whether he was having these experiences or if he was just plain crazy was far greater.

I cannot tell you how many new clients have said to me, "please tell me that I'm crazy so I can take medication or be hospitalized"! At least, they feel, a psychotic diagnosis would be a plausible explanation for what has been happening to them.

My clients are people who have gone through years of traditional therapy… have undergone a number of psychological tests and prescribed medication…and yet, the problem remains.

My clients come to me with symptoms of Post Traumatic Stress Disorder (PTSD) that is the result of a traumatic event. The Subconscious job is to protect us by blocking all or part of the event. They find it difficult to sleep through the night, concentrate on work or making through a normal day. Abductees/Experiencers are often hyper vigilant…with the sense that "something" is going to happen. Carrying around "the secret" becomes too much to bear and very often affects marriages and relationships with friends and family members.

Hypnotic regression brings forward buried memories/experiences where they are no longer mysterious or frightening. It's the bits and pieces or snatches of a memory since early childhood is what haunts the person causing them to question their own sanity. By the time they see me, they are ready to confront and deal with the information that their subconscious may bring forward. Once the buried memories come up to the surface the fear dissipates and the healing begins.

The longer I worked with Abductees/Experiencers, I realized that once my clients left my office, there were those who had no one else to talk to about their experiences and what occurred during their Hypnotherapy sessions. This realization prompted me to start a support group and in 1992, Close Encounter Resource Organization (CERO) was born. My goal was to provide a safe haven for like-minded people to share and discuss their lifelong experiences.

Since early childhood, Steve knew he was having experiences with entities he could not explain. I recall how apprehensive Steve was about pursuing hypnotic regression because of his wife's negative reaction to the subject of UFOs and alien beings. This reaction is not unusual for the partner or family member. However, Steve's strong determination prevailed and as a result, we developed a very long working relationship. He eventually became an integral member of CERO and like so many in the group have told me…"it feels like family" or "I have come home".

The more information that Steve was able to glean from his regressions was reflected in his artwork and sculptures from a very personal and deep level.

Steve's artistic talent and his many years working on major Hollywood films astounded me and I was honored when he offered his services as my "police artist" working with many of the CERO members. Several pieces of Steve's artwork have been featured in my lectures throughout the years as well as numerous television shows in the 1990s.

I am also proud to tell you that Steve's artwork is featured throughout my book, *Coronado: The President, The Secret Service and Alien Abductions* and my latest book, *Chosen: From The Alien Hybrid Program to the Fate of the Planet.*

Now all of these years later, Steve contacted me to tell me about his latest project, *But Something Is There* and how he wanted me and CERO members to be a part of it…I was overwhelmed with pride. As I read the treatment, it brought me back to working with Steve so intimately through hours and hours of hypnosis sessions, I can see, on a very personal level, how he has poured his heart and soul into *But Something Is There*…it brought tears to my eyes.

I am forever grateful to Steve for his trust and faith in my work and I thank him for his artistic contribution to not only the UFO community, but to his fellow CERO support group members.

For those of you who have been wondering and questioning your own experiences, whether or not they are real, through the pages of *But Something Is There,* my hope is that you will find your own answers and finally peace in your life.

- Yvonne Smith

Introduction

Allow me to attempt to explain how I perceive my own experience. As I am a bit of a closet scientist, it can be difficult at best. I grew up with the love of science and I still do love science. Any good scientist would not be convinced by just my opinion based on personal experience and little proof. I accept that. In fact I will always fight for their right to do so. This is what makes science, science.

I would ask anyone not to pre-judge me personally on reporting having these experiences. Based on hearsay of many people that claim these experiences, I can understand why you might.

So often the fringe, self titled "abductees" can be judgmental, fanatical, and obsessed even turning on the scientists that would question them about their experience. These same scientists that cured deceases and showed us the stars take it personally, their being doubted, that they lose their composure and react rather than responding to some honest, only curious, questions.

This may be well the reason that so many scientists discount looking any further into this phenomenon. If you claim an experience or contact with something or someone outside the realm of current perceptions of reality, you need to be intelligent about it, collected and calm. Report what you know, not what you believe; and show any evidence you may have. There is really little more one can do than that.

These same people can be convinced that they know what this experience is. They believe its aliens from another world. Also, they are being abducted against their will. They believe that the visitors are experimenting and harming our children. They give them names, names such as Grey's, Reptilians, Pleiadians and more.

I don't believe in any of these notions. In fact, I don't believe in anything at all. I prefer to know or not know things. But I never just believe. I'm OK with not knowing.

All I know is that I don't have mental illness. I don't have any medical conditions that would account for my experiences either. I am healthy and well. I have a good career and relationship with a beautiful woman. I have done lots of great things with my career. I have worked on many movies making creatures, space ships, props, costumes, filmmaking, visual effects, and more. I have been doing this work for a very long time.

I do have a certain measure of proof, eyewitnesses to some of these events, photographs, video, and strange foreign objects in my body. The bottom line is that I don't claim to know with what I'm dealing. It may come from my mind, or another dimension, a planet or universe. It appears to be highly intelligent and it interacts with me and has since I can remember.

I share this experience with millions of other people, some of whom I personally know. Mostly they don't write books or appear on talk shows but rather remain in the shadows. They know that they have far too much to risk in coming forward with this. I know, all too well, what can happen. It doesn't always, but it did to me.

I appeared on many talk shows. Sometimes I appeared on TV with my dear friend Whitley Strieber, Dr. Roger Leir, Yvonne Smith, and other notable people that either have had this experience or are brave enough to come forward about it.

During the Nineties, when I was at my peak with this experience, someone was stalking me. Whether it had been an agency, or someone private, or even the Visitors (as Whitley calls them), themselves, it remains to be seen. But many of these people claimed to be CIA, NSA and FBI.I had my mail withheld. It had been sent back to customers trying to buy my art. Customers got their mail and money returned with, "no such address." My phones were bugged. I was followed. I had my picture taken opening my front door, in restaurants and other locations by very official looking people, who would leave quickly. Sometimes they would jump into unmarked government cars. My friends reported seeing large objects hovering over my house. These people would hide in the bushes peep through my windows with ID badges that, when caught, would run for a car and leave. My family witnessed un-marked helicopters and harassment on numerous occasions, as I did. The list goes on and on.

In fact, one of the worst events with this type of activity was getting a call from the studios one day from one of the producers. She asked me if I was in trouble with the law? She explained that two very official-looking men with ID badges (they flashed) came in to the studio. They told her that it wasn't in their best interest to work with me. Needless to say, I was distressed. My late wife, Gilly was terrified. Maybe they were mistaken and had the wrong Ste-ve Neill. Who knows? There were many experienc-es, both shared, and alone, even accompanied by alleged Intelligence. I knew that this wasn't all just in my head. It's just not one of those things.

I know this all sounds like myth and fringe. It does and I agree. But it's important to note, that through time, many myths have become accepted as part of reality I cite the Mountain Gorilla. Like Bigfoot, they were considered fringe until 1902; then one was actually identified by German captain Rob-ert von Beringe. This is just one instance, out of many, where science didn't get it wrong, but didn't have the data to get it right.

So I'll share with you, without embellishing the memories and as best I can, my honest experience with this amazing phenomenon. It is an experience, or better still, journey. I don't have a name for it. I don't know what it is. And with real scientific inquiry it may one day be known. But something is there. The Visitor subject for many is a topic that is considered taboo. It's thought of as fringe, crazy, and without merit. My understanding is that people fear what they don't understand. It's like a dark room everyone is afraid to enter for fear of what they might find inside. What if there was something wonderful inside? In reality humans fear the unknown and the greatest unknown of them all is who we are or might be.

I do not and have not allowed that fear hold me back. Fear has held back the Human Race. It has kept us from evolving our consciousness. It has, for the most part, made us Earthbound in a huge universe that beckons us to commune with it.

If we will just look into the mirror and see ourselves, we just might find that we are the Visitors and have been all along. How amazing and impossible we are; yet we exist. And other impossible and amazing intelligences exist as well in our Universe. After all we are all children born of the stars.

Chapter One
The Lightning People

It was 1958 and I lived in an old flat with my parents in San Francisco on the Avenues.

The house was only a few blocks from the beach and, from there; I could hear the sounds of the sea and an amusement park called, "Play Land". I could see the rides from my window at night.

My parents both worked. I was surrounded by culture. My family was very creative and intelligent. Everyone could draw, play music, and paint. My mother's mom, my grandmother, was a genius photographer and chemist that worked for years with Ansel Adams. My dad was an amazing artist and engineer.

I was an only child and spent a lot of time alone. I had a nanny who lived in our flat. She took care of the house and me so my parents could work. The flat was large and was once a house, before it was converted to flats.

I can remember exactly when this all started. "What started", you may ask? My beginnings with, the unknown and the Visitor experience. How I saw it, at an early age, life was something more than what was perceived by my peers. Something told me that I was different.

As a child, I observed how other children and the adults behaved in their relationship to their reality. They never seemed to look up much, let alone look at the stars, as I did. I looked at the night sky often and wondered, "What's out there?" The night sky beckoned me.

Many of my peers had interests in playing baseball or another athletic activity. Few thought of doing more with their lives than had been done previously by their parents. They didn't dream much. But I wanted to be a scientist or artist. Sports never interested me. I wanted to study the stars and nature. I wanted to know all about the Cosmos.

I was interested in watching the space launches, looking through my telescope and reading science fiction. I loved movies about space travel. My heroes were pilots, scientist, artists and great thinkers like Einstein, Wernher von Braun, Chuck Yeager and more.

I loved music. Classical music was my favorite and Bach stirred my soul. His music called to me as the stars did at night. His music was the sound track of the stars. I had other favorites. My favorite symphony was "The Planets" by Holst. Beethoven's, "Moon Light Sonata", stirred my imagination of the mysterious night and the creatures that lived by night.

I wasn't afraid of the dark, either. I was more drawn by my curiosity to it. I found it magical.

My Dad and Mom were only married a short time before they divorced. Dad moved on and I lived with Mom. I only saw Dad on weekends.

Dad was an amazing artist and an engineer. My Mom was also talented as an artist and musician but choose to do office work as a way of supporting us. She worked hard and put aside her career desires.

I still remember in every detail my first day in kindergarten. I sat in that classroom and looked around at the other kids and felt a disassociation from them. I felt that there had been a mistake and I didn't belong there. I remained silent. Something was wrong.

One night it happened. Where we lived in San Francisco we were only a few blocks from the beach. I could see Playland from my window. I could hear clearly, from my bed, the sounds of the night there. I could hear seals on the Cliff House. I could hear the ocean and its foghorns and ships.

I lived on 47th Avenue in the city but on that night I was awoken by an absolute silence. You wouldn't think that such peace wouldn't be wakening but it was so out of the norm that it woke me right up.

I felt a presence. Something was there. I looked around the room. It was late, 3:00 am. And then a beam of light appeared in the room silently searching. It was followed by another and then another. They were beams.

Anyone today would consider the source was a helicopter. But in the late 50's we didn't have police helicopters and certainly not helicopters that were completely silent. The silence was deafening.

I wasn't frightened as much as profoundly curious. What and who was doing this? I slowly crawled out of bed and onto the floor. I crawled on my hands and knees. I made my way to the windowsill. I stayed in the shadows of the wall, as not to be seen.

When I got to the windowsill, I slowly raised up to get a peek over the edge. What I saw was a near-blinding light source coming from high up. As I viewed it, the light immediately shifted its attention to me. It appeared to be searching for me. This startled me so much that I ducked down below the sill. I looked for a place to hide in my room. I saw my desk and made a run for it. I hid under the desktop. Now I was a bit frightened. There was something intelligent behind those lights and they had just found me.

I thought I'd be safe under the desk. That they would never see me there, but the lights somehow found their way into my room. They lowered down to find me under the desk. Now, I was truly frightened. The lights seem to fill the room. It wasn't long before I started to notice movement in the lights. These shadows had form. The forms had very thin and finely boned humanoid figures, small, agile with enlarged heads. I could only make out the silhouettes of two figures.

They approached me and, as they did, I heard a voice in my mind, not with my ears. It was feminine, soft and breathless, "Don't be afraid."

The next morning I woke up on the floor in front of my parents' bed. In the past, if I had nightmares, they didn't want me to crawl into bed with them; so I would sleep in front of the bed, out of their view, on a carpet in front of the bed. I would sneak back into my room in the morning.

I was sure then, as I am today that this wasn't a dream. It was totally different and I would remember it in detail. But there were these blackout periods in the experience I would, later in life, try to uncover.

I didn't tell anyone about what had happened. I was smart enough to know at that age that I might be considered to have mental illness. Or just be told it wasn't real and that I have an active imagination. I did have an active imagination make no doubt about that. I was a creative child. But I would never have conjured up such a scenario as this.

Although I was very interested in science fiction, TV, movies and books, I never once, back then, thought that I might be having visitations from aliens from another world. I did then, as I do today, have no real idea what happened. I knew in my heart it wasn't a dream. I knew the difference. All I knew is something very real happened to me.

I thought I was alone with all of this. However, later in life, I would find I wasn't alone nor was this experience unique to me alone.

Over time I had many such experiences as a child. I called them the lightning people. I thought of them as fairies or little people, even doctors. My parents would take me on trips to visit family friends and, more than once on overnight stay, these things would happen there too. I would always keep silent about it. I lived in a secret world of wonder. Through those experiences, I felt something or someone was trying to touch me.

Chapter Two
My Grandfather

My parents often sent me to my grandparents' house for the weekend. It was a small town in Marin County, called Santa Venetia, just outside of San Rafael. They lived in a quaint little house, in the countryside with rolling hills and starry nights.

I loved visiting them. I loved the countryside. The stars at night were so much more than I could see in the City of San Francisco. It was there, for the very first time, that I saw the Milky Way. I knew then that everyone one of those pinpoints of light was another sun. It stirred me with wonder.

There was an Air Force base close by. I could walk to it from the house. I would walk over and sit by the chain link fence and watch the F-86s and T-33s flying. I loved flying, jets, planes and rockets.

My Grandfather was a quiet man. He was Irish born and raised. He worked at a bank for years. I really didn't know much about him. He hardly spoke. My Grandmother was quite the opposite. She was over-bearing, ultra-liberal and very outspoken. Their relationship was strange at best. They didn't talk much and disagreed on so many issues. They had a son, my uncle, who was only 4 years older than me. He was a problem child. He was always in trouble and not very respectful of his father. He and Grandmother treated Grandfather poorly to say the least. They made fun of him in front of me and it was discomforting at best.

Grandfather spoke of his experiences to me about growing up in Ireland. He experienced so many things, from little people to the Banshee, and he was dead serious about it. I knew he had experienced these things. I could see it in his eyes. But, Grandmother at length, would make fun of him and my uncle would tease him too. I knew he was telling the truth, and once, while walking one evening, I had a close encounter with him.

Grandfather's house was the last house on the block. It faced an old farmer's field and the open countryside beyond. There was a dirt frontage road where we would take walks in the evening to look at the stars.

On one night, I clearly remember, we went out to see Sputnik. It was 1957. San Rafael and the lights of San Francisco were far enough way and so much less in those days that the Milky Way sprawled out before us as we walked down the dirt road. The crickets and other night noises surrounded us in a magical evening full of wonder.

Grandfather always brought his binoculars with him and would show me points of interest in the night sky. One night it was a moonless and ultra dark. There weren't many aircraft back then moving across the sky, as there are today. Not even the nearby air force base was flying any aircraft that night. I noticed the moving star first, as I recall. I asked Grandfather if that might be Sputnik. As it turned out, it was. In this time we had no other satellites orbiting the Earth. It had to be. I watched with amazement. The thought that something human beings had created was now in space orbiting our planet. I knew this was the beginning to a grand adventure.

We watched as it headed off over the horizon. Then I noticed another moving star. This one was red-colored and moved differently than the satellite. It sort of wavered in the sky and seemed to be coming straight for us. I knew about meteors and asked Grandfather if it were one. He didn't know and was unsure, but supposed it could have been. It kept getting closer and bigger toward us.

It was about that time I noticed the deafening silence all around us. The sounds of the night were gone as before. The star was looking more like a meteor as it approached, but it wasn't moving very fast. It appeared to be slowing down. It was a round sphere that appeared on fire with slight flames licking its surface. As it neared, it hovered over us. The ball hovered for a brief time and then slowly moved off down the frontage road and into the distance. It sped up until it vanished.

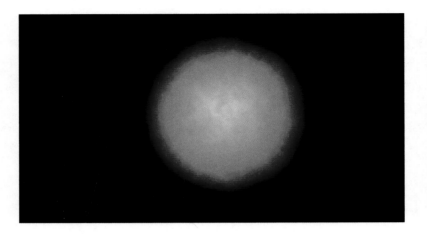

We returned back to the house and sat in the dining room and discussed what we had just have seen. Grandfather felt somehow that it connected with us. It knew we were there. That's when Grandmother came into the room. She had over-heard our conversation and commented.

She made fun of Grandfather. She told him to stop making me think I saw anything more than a meteor. This bothered me. I had been there and had seen the object. Grandmother didn't and yet she chooses to pass judgment. She snidely com-mented that Grandfather claimed to see lots of things. She made jokes about the Leprechauns. But I stood up for him and told her no. We saw it. It wasn't a meteor and it was real.

When I spent the night at their house, I slept in Grandfather's study. It was a little room with a win-dow over his desk. I slept on a small couch in the room that they made up as a bed. As I sat on the edge of the bed, ready to sleep for the night, Grandfather came in to tell me a story. An experience he had in Ireland.

One night he was taking his mother home. They were in a horse drawn carriage. He often did this and on this particular night they tried to cross in front of the old church, as they always had, but on this night the horse protested. Something frightened it. Grandfather stopped the carriage and got out to investigate. The church was an old stone church with a yard to the side of its entrance. The front of the church faced forward. It was L-shaped to the right; in this expanse there were trees and brushes that hide much of the yard in the dark night. What-ever was disturbing the horse was in there.

Grandfather decided to walk into the churchyard; as he did, he could just make out a man sitting in the corner of the church, where the L-shape met. There was a slight ledge there and the man was sit-ting on it in the shadows. He approached slowly, with caution. As he got closer, he could see the man was wearing a long coat and a brimmed hat. It ap-peared to be forties-style. It was strange because this was in the early 1900's. He couldn't make out his face at all. He was looking down and his legs were crossed. When Grandfather looked down at the man's feet, what frightened him the most was that they were hooves. Upon seeing this, he looked up at the man again and the man lifted his head to look at Grandfather.

Grandfather thought he saw the devil himself. His face was long and bony. His eyes were large, slanted, dark and lifeless. With this, Grandfather backed away and ran back to the carriage. He sped off into the night for fear for his life.

When Grandfather told me this story I could see the look of fear in his eyes. He clearly experienced something that was very real to him. Misinterpreted? Maybe. However, it was no less real. Later in my life experience, I would come to experience and know things that related back to his experience, without the culture and folklore of old Ireland. He didn't see the Devil but something else.

I had other experiences with Grandfather during those summers in Marin County. It was told that the farmer who owned the field beyond that same dirt road fell down the well and died. His ghost was seen walking around the old well as a spectral image by the locals.

On another night, while out on an evening walk with Grandfather, I notice peripherally a glowing light to my right. When I turned to look at the source, I saw this man. He was softly lighted and he shimmered as he moved. It wasn't like he was walking, but floating and, as he did, he rippled. I pointed it out to Grandfather and we both watched in silence. He slowly faded away and vanished. On this night, when we went back to the house, we didn't dare speak of what we had seen. Now these may seem like two different phenomenon, but again, through my experience in the years to come, I would find they were both deeply connected.

I experienced and learned so many things living those weekends and summers at my Grandparents'. I feel that I plugged into my connection with the Universe and nature like I never could have living in the city. I craved that connection and the stars at night.

Sleeping in Grandfather's study was kind of creepy. There was a streetlight outside that shined into the room and lit it up enough to remind me of the lights coming into my room in San Francisco. On the walls were many pictures and Grandfather's family crest. There was also a picture of my great, great, great grandmother who was a full Black Feet American Indian. She had haunting eyes that seemed to stare at me.

One night at Grandfather's, I awoke to the silence once more and there was someone at the side of my bed trying to wake me. I heard a woman's voice as she tugged at the covers telling me to wake up. I finally turned over to look at her. She was a very small being. I want to say she had a large head, but to be truthful, my memory of her is vague. I do remember her being very small; and she was backlit by that streetlight.

The being awakened me. She told me that someone was waiting for me in the backyard and that we had to go there. We walked down the hallway towards the dining room. There were sliding glass doors there that lead to the backyard. It was very dark in the house as we walked through it. As we got to the sliding glass door, I expected it to be opened by her but instead she took my arm and, somehow, which is hard to explain, we passed right through it. I could just feel a slight tug on my body as we did.

Then we were outside. There were many of these small people outside in the yard. They all seemed busy and didn't really notice me. We walked to the center of the yard. I could see the stars. So many stars that the sky had a glow about it. Then I saw it. There was a dark circle passing slowly in front of the stars like a black hole in the sky moving towards us. She told me to stay still and not to be afraid. No one was going to hurt me. I wasn't really afraid. I was curious and mystified to say the least.

As it came closer, I could just make out a lighting effect at the edge of this disc-shaped object. The rim seemed very reflective or mirrored. But the center was pitch black. When it was right over us, it started to light up from the inside. It looked like an opening of a door with a light beam behind it. This beam came down on us. It wasn't really bright but bright enough that, when I looked down at the small being next to me, I could see her better. She was small, finely boned and had a large head with black slanted eyes. She really wasn't frightening looking. She wasn't threatening at all. She pointed up and, as she did, I felt my body become weightless and we started to float up towards the object. As we came close to the object, it seemed massive. Although the outer edges of the disc seemed metallic and highly reflective, there was nothing but blackness at its center except for this sort of doorway. We came closer to the doorway and I could see movement. There were other small beings waiting. When we got right up to them, I felt as though I passed through a doorway. There was an odd feeling like I had just entered another realm. Once inside, we were in a corridor. It seemed very long as though we were in some kind of huge building or facility. It looked like the walls, floors and ceilings were made of stainless polished steel. There was, what looked like bulkheads, which were evenly spaced.

The small beings moved me along down the hallway and, as they did, I could see inside the many doorways that lead to rooms off the hallway.

Inside I could just make out tables with people lying on the tables. There were small beings all around them; some were taller and shaped differently. They took me into one of these rooms and laid me on a table. They were gentle and all the time telling me that I wouldn't be harmed; they just needed to examine me and make some tests. They also told me I was special, important to them, even different from the others. I was never sure what they meant by that; and, until this day, all I can do is guess. All the time this was happening I wasn't under restraint. I seemed to do this willingly. It had happened before. While lying on the table, I looked around the room. The other people lying on the table were naked and unconscious. The small beings were very busy using instruments on them and doing what looked like an examination.

I felt somewhat altered. Even remotely drugged but I could never be entirely sure. A being approached me and this one was like the others, only taller. The being had the large eyes that were entirely black; I thought I could see eyes behind them like sunglasses on a human being. The being was tall, thin, with an enlarged head that was bald. It had a pointed chin and little openings for a nose and thin fine lips. She (and that what I concluded based on the sound of her voice) spoke to me. She never moved her mouth and once again the sound or (lack of sound) seemed to be in my mind. In my mind I heard, "Don't be afraid". To be honest I was a bit afraid at this moment. She wasn't like the others and seemed very much in control. As she bent over and approached me, close up to my face, I felt the ability to control my body fade. I couldn't move. She came to within an inch or two of my eyes and stared into me. She spoke again. "You are our child, you are our hope".

Then I started to have visions of this vast void of stars, galaxies and nebula. I moved through them as if I was disembodied. My emotions swelled with wonder and joy. I was escalated and began to cry. I felt so connected, in love and I never wanted to leave. All the time this was happening, I knew the smaller beings were doing something to me. I didn't know what it was and I didn't care. Everything faded for me. The last thing I remember was coming to and seeing the tall beautiful being looking into my eyes as she stepped back. She seemed to smile or I felt it from her. I felt deep love for her.

The next thing I can recall is being placed back in my bed. The little being walked away into the dark of the hallway and was gone. My memory the next morning was reality changing. The world, my reality seemed so different. I concluded, at this young age, that it must have been a dream. But I knew deep inside it wasn't. I was a very lucid dreamer. I could almost always remember my dreams in vivid detail. I could change things in the dreams and often I knew when was dreaming. This was different. In years to come, I would find out I wasn't the only one.

I spent many summers at both my grandparent's homes, my Dad's and my Mom's. I had many such experiences. Sometimes, with other children who were scared to death. But what happened to them and later in life they would not remember.

Chapter Three
Mr. Lee

An early memory from my days in the first house we lived, in San Francisco, was our gardener, Mr. Lee. It has been so long but I distinctly remember him. He was a very small Asian man. He seemed very old, judging by the lines on his face. In hindsight, he today reminds me of Yoda.

Mr. Lee visited us every week and attended the backyard. The backyard was a pretty open space and toward the back, it had a thicket that was dense with foliage and overgrown. I used to play in there; it was like having my own secret forest. It was a wonderland of insects, lizards and nature.

Mr. Lee fascinated me. I loved to ask him questions about things we would see in the garden and we would talk about the world and space. He seemed to know a lot about everything and I was always curious to know. He would answer all my questions, and always, he had a recurring theme in his lessons, "We are all connected." He taught me that every living thing and person across the expanse of the Universe was connected. He taught me that all life was sacred. He also told me that the human race was disconnecting from nature and the Universe in a quest for greed and power. This would not end well if the course was not changed. He told me that we were destroying the environment, and in doing so, we were unknowingly destroying our future and ourselves.

When he would tell me these things, it was often in the green light of the trees and foliage; this light made him look green himself. Thinking back now, he was odd looking. He may not have been a human in the classic sense. Later in my teens I would be told these same things once again.

Years later, in talking to Mom, I brought him up to her. There was a long pause and then she told me that we had never had an Asian gardener. I was surprised because I could remember him so well. However, she flatly denied we ever had a gardener at all. I don't know how I could have been mistaken. I have a very good memory and I never forget a face or an event of any kind. I have been told this by Mary, my late wife Gilly and friends for years. I have a photographic memory. Even as I write this, I can see him in every detail, as if it happened yesterday.

In years to come I would read Whitley's Strieber's book, "The Key". What really caught my attention about the book was the little man that spoke to Whitley. Was this his Mr. Lee? In reading the book it was very reminiscent of my Mr. Lee.

Another experience I had reading "The Key" was that every time Whitley would ask the man a question, I knew the answer before I read it. It was as though I had been told the very same things all those years ago.

I'll never know whether Mr. Lee was a childhood fantasy, however remembering it now, I can tell you from my heart that it was very real.

I remember clearly in the thicket of the backyard his looking so green that it was like looking at Yoda. He told me that I was different than other children and that the things we talked about I would have to be careful expressing to other kids or even adults. Discussing such things could bring unwanted attention to me and they would question my sanity. He also told me that I would know a kindred spirit when I met one. He told me to be careful in questioning authority. Authority that often wasn't justified, but rather taken. Leading my life in secret was something that was necessary or I may become subject to scrutiny, or bullied and harmed by the fearful and ignorant. I was different. In the years to come, through my experience, I would hear this told to me time and time again by these beings.

I always looked forward to Mr. Lee and his visits and then one day, like all things, he wasn't there anymore. I always wondered what happened to him. I have often thought of him and his strange face in the thicket. The knowledge he imparted on to me about the Universe, my life and the world will never be forgotten.

So who was Mr. Lee? Was he an imaginary friend? Was he our gardener that Mom forgot? I guess we'll never know.

This takes me back to Whitley's book, "The Key". When you read this book, then you'll know where I'm going. However, if you haven't, the short story, I can tell you that Whitley was staying in a hotel during a book tour. Late at night a knock came on his door and this little man entered his room to have a talk with Whitley.

This man, whom he didn't know, who came into his room, disturbed Whitley. Whitley even thought about calling security until the man began to speak. As he spoke, Whitley heard him say things that told him this was part of the Visitor Experience.

I wonder if my Mr. Lee was my little man who imparted on me many of the same lessons and stories.

Chapter Four
The G-Men

While living in the flat on 47th Avenue.in San Francisco, many interesting days and nights occurred. I'm not going into every single detail and account, but it suffices to say those early years between 6 and 12 years of age were busy. I will attempt to detail some of the more interesting experiences that I had in those days, the ones that really stand out.

I had a step-grandfather whom I loved very much. He was a brilliant scientist. He visited us often and was my favorite grandfather. When he visited, he always gave me lots of attention and spent quality time with me. He always engaged me, and my questions about science and space, my favorite subject. More than anyone else in my family, including my dad and mom, I had his attention. He admired my curiosity. He pleaded with my parents to get me a telescope. Finally years later my dad did get me a telescope.

I remember well his apartment in Berkeley. The place was organized, neat, and clean. It had amazing black and white prints of the galaxies and nebula framed on the walls. Grandfather Carnahan wore thick glasses and always wore a white shirt and a tie. His pockets had pens in them and he carried a slide rule. Grandfather Carnahan worked at Berkeley in the laboratories and was developing the first camera to photograph the splitting of an atom. He worked on the Linear accelerator. He was one of those genius kids drafted out of high school, during the Second World War, to work on the Manhattan project. As a result, he never got to go to college for his degree. I searched the net trying to find a picture of him. I found this one taken in 1947. He is the 10th person from the left. He is named in the article too. The following url goes directly to the article: www.symmetrymagazine.org/article/august-200...

Mom used to talk proudly of his work at Berkeley. Unfortunately, he was never given credit for his invention of the camera that took the first pictures of the splitting of the atom. Berkeley never gave him his promised PHD. This later broke his heart. During the late 50s he's was always at our home for parties and events.

This is where, what I called the G-Men, came into the picture. They used to sit outside the house and watch the place. Mom talked about them and even a few times invited them in. As far as I was told, it was because of my Grandfather's secret work that they were sent there to watch us.

Remember that this was during a very sensitive period in our country. It was the McCarthy Era and there was a commie under every rock. My parents were progressive and they had friends that were considered bohemian, even beatniks. My grandmother was a brilliant chemist and photographer who, at that time, worked for her dear friend, Ansel Adams. They knew artists and musicians of all kinds. My family was all talented artists and musicians themselves. Dad was like a human camera and could draw anything he saw to photo-real levels. Mom played piano and also was a very good illustrator. I could go on at length, however, at that time, free thinkers and artists were all under suspicion with the Feds.

But now I wonder. Were the G-Men there because of my experiences? In exploring my experiences, I have come to know many others with this experience who have the same backgrounds and such experiences with men in suits and black cars.

Much later, in my 30's and 40's, I would come to experience this again and on a much more intense level. But I will go over that in a later chapter.

During this time, I often noticed, both in my experience and in daily life, the appearance of strange men in long coats and 40's style brimmed hats. They seemed to stalk me and in my experiences they were there too, always watching. Years later I would learn about the men in black. Were they the men in black? I will never know but I can tell you with honesty, they were there and I saw them.

Chapter Five
More Bumps in Night

When I was 8 years old my parents divorced. I remember Mom telling me that Dad wouldn't be living with us anymore. I was pretty upset. A dark day made even worse by the news that I wouldn't be going with Dad but instead staying with Mom.

I never had a great relationship with my Mom. She was very intelligent, pretty and wise, however, she lacked something very important: affection. She never hugged me and often blamed and punished me for things I didn't do. She was a big fan of corporal punishment. She was very hard on me. When I visited my friends' homes I saw how their parents were loving, kind and compassionate, I knew then, being a smart kid, that Mom had issues.

By contrast my Dad was very compassionate and affectionate. He would come on weekends and take me to Marin County to stay with him or his mother, out in the country, the place where I encountered the red ball.

After they split up, Mom rented another flat only a few doors away from the old one. This place was a bit more modern and we lived upstairs. We lived where I could go anywhere, from Golden Gate Park to downtown. The park was within walking distance. I had a bike and I would ride there all the time. One of my favorite haunts was the lake, where I could watch the model sailboats and fish for crawdads and carp. Also nearby, were the Cliff House and the ruins of the old Cliff House that burned down years ago where I would often play. There were coastal bunkers still there from WW2 I would enter and explore. My school, Lafayette Gamer School was within in a few miles and I walked or road there alone every day. Everything was close by. Though the city was a wonderland, I always preferred the countryside. There I could experience nature and the stars.

Shortly after we moved to the new place, I had another experience. I was lying in my bed trying to sleep and I had this nagging urge that something was wrong or about to happen. I was sleeping with one eye open, as they would say, but soon I drifted off. I felt a motion and weightlessness; then I felt cool and the temperature dropped. I opened my eyes and to my amazement I was outside looking straight up at the foggy sky and I was approaching the fog. I panicked and could only move my head. I looked down to see my street, the cars parked on it and the streetlights. Then it hit me. I could see my bike. I had left it outside and was so worried someone would take it. I thought maybe I might be having a flying dream. I had plenty of them but I could always control my flight and I had no ability to do now. I couldn't move much at all and I was going higher and higher every second. As I passed through the fog, I felt a presence next to me and as I looked over I could see one of the beings. She told me, again, "Don't be afraid".

She pointed up and, as I looked up, I could see the stars and something round and dark in the middle of them. I saw a disc-shaped black hole. As we grew closer, I could see light or some type of reflection occurring on its rim. I can only describe it as some kind of door opening in the middle of the blank disc. I could tell because it was backlit by soft amber light. A beam of soft blue light emerged from it and fell on us lighting the way. As we approached closer, I could see over beings near the opening and a soft warm amber light came from inside. The object close-up was just black, lacking light all together. As we passed through the opening or door, we entered a hallway. There were arched ceilings and walls that slanted a bit. I had seen this all before. I had no idea where I was, a building, some kind of craft? My feeling was that this was another place a structure, not a craft. As we moved down the hallway, I was aware of doorways to the right and left of me and inside there were rooms. I could just glimpse inside and I could see more beings and people lying on their backs on metal tables. It was quiet, very little sound and the temperature was cool. They took me into one of these rooms and sat me on a table. The table felt cool and the beings were buzzing about attending to other people there. Most were not clothed. Some in night clothes others in daily wear. It was hard to get a good look at them because the beings kept me distracted. Always having my attention and telling me that they wouldn't hurt me. They laid me down and, as I lay there, I was well aware I couldn't move freely. I wasn't really afraid. It was as if this was routine and it made sense somehow.

The ceiling had a curve to it and overhead lights. There were beams running across the ceiling that were also present in the hallways. There was some kind of equipment too that had cables with instruments hanging from the ceiling and against the walls panels with colored lights. As I lay there, two of the beings came to either side of me. They told me again not to be afraid. Suddenly, a much taller being came into view and towered over me. It looked different from the smaller creatures. The face was a bit more human and a large bald head, pointed chin and large eyes, that where so dark, they were nearly black. I could just get the sense that there was an iris and a pupil because I could see movement as if behind sunglasses. The skin color was closer to a flesh color and not so gray as the smaller ones. It leaned over me, came in so close to my face it was starting to get uncomfortable. It stopped coming closer and then I heard a voice in my head. "You are different from the others, special. You are not like them." The voice was distinctly female, soft, breathless and calming. She seemed familiar and I felt an emotion towards her. This hadn't been the first time we had met. Although I really didn't know what she meant, I did feel it. This was apparent the first day in grammar school, when I looked around the classroom and felt there had been some kind of mistake. I wasn't supposed to be here. Just being on Planet Earth felt wrong, as though I had come from somewhere else. This world just seemed backwards to me as a child, less technologically advanced, even primitive. I never understood how one could feel this way if we were to believe what science had taught us. I surely must be just crazy. But was I? She placed her hand on my forehead and I felt warmth from her touch. My mind filled with a montage of imagery. I saw planets, space, and even other worlds with civilizations far more advanced than ours. It was as though I was connected to her and sharing her memories and experiences. It was literally being downloaded to my mind. She smiled and I closed my eyes and slipped into a sleep only to wake the next morning in my bed, as though it never happened.

At this age I knew it could have just been all a dream. But I also knew I dreamed it before. Each time it was different but the same beings and places. It felt real and these weren't dreams I forgot. I knew something special was happening to me. I also knew how I would be perceived, if I dare speak of it. So I didn't. I kept it to myself. My world was different. I walked in a different, maybe even a more honest, perception of reality than most of the inhabitants of this planet. Was this what she meant?

Then I remembered my bike! I got out of bed, looked out the window and down on the street where I had left it. It was gone. I was very upset about the bike. Mom berated me for being so careless. She never gave me another bike. I had to buy my own.

Chapter Six
Night School

Another memory I have is a strange one to be sure. As I learned more about my experience in later days, I found out it wasn't unique to me alone. For as long as I thought it was a dream, (or more to the point, I was hoping it was all a dream) and to be honest, this was more frightening then the experience with the beings. Late at night I'd be awakened and told to go with these men. They looked much like the G-Men. They would rush me off to a car parked outside and take me to my grammar school, only a mile or so away from our flat. When we arrived, the school was dark and creepy. There were other sedans parked outside. I could see other kids being ushered into the school by these G-men types in suits and with brimmed hats. Most of them were in nightclothes and robes as I was.

Inside the school we were taken into the main hallways and told to stand in line. They had flashlights and there were some dim lights inside some of the rooms. I could just see this through the open doors. There were adults in lab coats moving about, in and out of the rooms. We were all told to remove our clothes. This I did not like, standing there with all these other naked boys. If there were girls, they must have been in another part of the school. The treatment was cold. These adults were cold and although I couldn't be sure, it seemed as though most of the kids were not fully with it, I felt drugged. But I wasn't. Again I was treated differently and I don't know why.

We were eventually, one by one, brought into a room and examined. The examination was pretty routine stuff. Open your mouth and say ah. They took our blood pressure and the other unpleasant procedures, like a rectal exam. Then they did something really disturbing. We were given this shot in the arm. But it was in the part of the arm where the lower limb and upper met on the inside. I remember it burning really bad and they left the needle in for a long time before removing it. After all this, we were told to put our cloths back on, go back in the hallway and stand in line.

Later we were filed into a classroom full of kids. There was a big screen over a blackboard and we were shown images and given a lecture. But to this day, I have little memory of what we were told or shown. Maybe this was due to the fact I was so frightened or maybe a result of the shot we were given. My gut feeling is that we were being asked more than told about our experiences and the beings. Images come to mind of the beings and, some of the images were associated with their behavior. Why was this happening to us? They seemed very concerned and at the same time and they were being very cautious with us, even paranoid.

Later we would be taken back to our homes and put back in our bedrooms. We would easily fall back to sleep. It was more like blacked-out from whatever they gave us. When I woke up in the morning it all seemed like a bad dream. My arm hurt and I felt drugged. I couldn't be sure if Mom knew something about it or not. How else could they have come late at night and not be seen or heard. There were times she took me to doctors and some of the same things were done to me. None it seemed right or even routine. This all continued for a couple more years.

In 1962 we moved to Sharp Park Pacifica, California, 20 miles or more down the coast from San Francisco. The city was more of a small coastal town where Mom had bought a house. For a while things seemed quiet. I went to elementary school, met some nice friends and started enjoying a new life. I continued looking to the skies. In the back of my mind, I knew I was different and someone out there had a vested interest in me. Still, I filed it away in my mind under unknown, maybe dreams, maybe something else; I dared not contemplate. I never told anyone about it, not my family or even my best friends.

Chapter Seven

Watching the Skies

I liked living in Pacifica. There were more stars and natural countryside. All the things I loved. Dad got me a refractor telescope and I used to put it out on the porch at night and look at the planets and stars. We lived at the foot of a tall hill where, at the top, was a Nike base. I remember sometimes seeing the missiles sticking up out of the ground atop the hill. My friends and I used to play on that hill and hike up there but when you looked through the chain-link fence, all you could see was an open field of tall grass. The missiles were hidden underground. Below them was an old WW2 bunker. This one was huge and although they had chained up the entrance, you could crawl down the air vents and get inside. It was several stories once inside. This old structure still had rooms with old equipment in them. It was dug deep into the hillside and completely abandoned. In fact, the whole hillside had gun bunkers that used to watch the coastline during the war.

Sometimes at night, I'd be looking at the stars and would notice strange lights in the sky and even lights that moved over the base. On one such night, I had my friend from across the street spending the night. I often talked about UFOs with Mike and he had an interest in them too. I told him if I ever saw one I'd show him. That night I awakened and found myself standing on the back porch. I didn't know how I had got there but I looked up at the base on top the hill and there was this eerie hat shaped light over the base. Then it silently moved down the steep hillside. I got so excited I ran into the house, woke up Mike and literally dragged him outside to see it.

The hill was quite steep and there were no roads in front of it. There was no way a vehicle could be there or driven down the hill. But this amber colored hat-shaped light kept coming closer and closer all in perfect silence. Mike was in a dazed state and not really excited about it. He just wanted to go back to sleep. As I followed him into my bedroom, Mom woke up and asked why we were up. She said it's 3:00 in the morning and to go to bed. I told her we had seen a UFO and she told me there weren't any UFOs; that is all nonsense. Go to bed. Mike got in his sleeping bag but I went to the porch again. It was gone.

The next morning Mom was up and at the kitchen table having her morning coffee. Sitting there next to her was our local newspaper, The Pacifica Tribune. She hadn't read it yet. As she picked it up and started reading, her face went blank. She looked at me and handed me the paper. The story on the front page was about a UFO that was sighted over the Nike base during the night. She never talked to me about it again.

I have tried to locate the Pacifica Tribune archives online but have been unsuccessful. I may have to visit them and look at actual records one day. I remember it clearly. There was a UFO that night. I couldn't remember if something more happened that night, but it may have. Waking up on the porch was a dead giveaway. I would have known if I were a sleepwalker. Mike and I continued to watch the skies and look for UFOs often. We were kids and it was a fun thing to do. But I never told him about my encounters or sneaking out late at night.

I was and am a big Batman fan. I made my own costume and made Mike a Robin costume. We went out for Halloween and sometimes, just at night, we'd sneak out in costume for fun from the downstairs Bat Cave, as I would call it.

I started going to the library and read more and more about the subject of UFOs. I loved watching "Twilight Zone" and" the Outer Limits". It was about that time that one of my favorite shows started. It was called "the Invaders". Little did I know that in the future I would work on seven motion pictures for Larry Cohen, the creator of the TV series.

Chapter Eight
Night Meetings

Our basement had a large living room with a bar. There were bunk beds and an adjoining bathroom. My favorite part there was a 90-gallon fish tank built into the wall. I loved to spend time down there by myself. This is what I, in the previous chapter, called "The Bat Cave".

Often, Mom would leave town for summer vacation and my Aunt Hazel would stay with me. I would spend most of my after-school time there, reading books and my favorite Batman comics. Aunt Hazel was a wonderful and beautiful woman; so vastly talented and a fine artist. I loved spending time with her. She gave me my freedom. She wasn't judgmental and would talk to me about everything.

Our house, as I said before, was at the foot of the Nike base hill. Across the street was a row of houses that sat at the base of that steep hill. Behind those houses, up high, at the foot of the hill was a plateau. It had been leveled at one time most likely to build a structure. To this day nothing has been built there. I played there all the time. One night I was sleeping downstairs in the basement when I felt this urge to go there. I was scared to death to go out in the dark this late at night, but the urge was so overwhelming that I did. It was a challenge, a dare if you will. I'd put on my clothes and sneak out and go up there.

Once there, I can remember being scared, but steadfast to stay. It was dark and completely silent. This is where things get fuzzy. I can't seem to remember what happened next. I have a recollection of people wearing dark pointed hoods and dark robes. I can remember a dark object hovering in the sky close to the ground. Unlike other experiences, I'm lacking information, and this is where hypnosis can and has helped me. One day I'll venture into this more and it's enough to say that when I read my dear friend Whitley Strieber's book, "The Secret School", it gave me chills. Whitley, as a boy, sneaked out into the night also to meet with Visitors at an old tree. We seemed to parallel often in our experience and today it comes as no surprise.

About this time, I started paying a lot more attention to UFO's. Mike and I would crawl up on to his roof at night and watch the skies for activity with binoculars. We saw a lot of strange lights and fast moving objects. Even back then, I knew enough about our aircraft to know the difference.   I loved airplanes, jets and rockets and I knew what they looked like and the lights they should have. Few of the objects I saw in those days fit the criteria for human aircraft. I started visiting the local library to find books on the subject and I found a few. I read George Adamski's books on his experiences. I read Keyhoe's books and more. I read lots of books about space travel and astronomy. I spent a lot of time building model rockets.

I watched many science fiction movies and I had favorites such as "Earth vs. the Flying Saucers", "The Day the Earth Stood Still", and "Destination Moon". In fact, I was a super George Pal fan and loved all his movies. I watched Disney's "Man in Space" series and dreamed of going to space one day. It was all in my heart and soul. My passion, I believe, came from my experiences.

Of all the things I saw and read, "The Interrupted Journey" by Barney and Betty Hill, about their famous encounter, was the one that really grabbed me. Although I was never stopped on the road in the country at night, or been abducted at that time, I could relate so deeply to what I was reading. It gave me chills. It all felt too familiar. I would later face a similar journey on a dark road at night.

Chapter Nine
Burney, California

    I spent some of my summers in Burney, California. Burney is a small logging town high in the mountains in far Northern California. My grandmother on my Mom's side lived there. She was the local lumber mill photographer and ran the lab there. Once I spent a full year there once. I attended the local school and met my first girlfriend. All this time I felt this presence watching and caring for me.

    Burney was in the middle of nowhere. There were rich forests and mountains. This was a wonderland for me. I started going there when I was 10. I would wander in the forests all day by myself with only my dog and cork shotgun to protect me all day. I would go fishing for hours on Burney Creek and watch the stars at night. It was very dangerous for a 10-year-old boy all by himself. I'd go deep into the forest and catch snakes and lizards. The reptiles, frogs, turtles, birds and big scary bugs fascinated me. On one of my many outings, I was on a fire trail, between the tall trees, when a mountain lion crossed my path only a few feet away. I stood motionless. The cat just looked at me for a moment. It was if we had connected (we did actually and I would learn this one day). We had this moment of eye contact. After a moment he just moved on across the road and into the forest. I was lucky. I had other such encounters with bears and other animals. I often ran into deer and it was always the same. We'd look at each other, share the moment and move on. It was a real gift that I am grateful for every day I live. I had so many times been in a situation where things could have gone horribly wrong, yet they never did.

I have memories I never explored later in life. Most of my encounters I could remember all the details but many others I still cannot. One such broken memory was riding at night in the back seat of Grandmother's car. Grandfather Carnahan and Grandmother drove along this dark road at night where we encountered a group of people and lights. They appeared to be working on the road. It appeared to be road construction. We started to slow down, as we approached, and eventually stopped. There was a large vehicle over to the left side of the road and all these people holding lights. I remember a lot of road workers and they were wearing metal hard hats. (As I write this I feel an anxiety, even a little queasy, which is surprising after all these years. What I have been finding, as I write this book, is that many memories I thought were blocked are coming out in the process of writing about them.) One of the men came to the driver's side and started talking to Grandfather. I couldn't really make out everything he said. He told us that we would be detained for a while and asked us to get out of the car. He opened the car door and then two more people opened the other doors and helped us out of the car. I remember feeling unsettled by this. Something was very wrong. I looked at Grandmother and she looked like a zombie. She was blanked-faced and so was Grandfather. They escorted us across the road to the large vehicle on the side of the road. The lights on the vehicle were very bright so it was hard to make out its exact shape. There was a door and it was open. They walked us inside. I remember it being quiet inside. They walked my grandparents off to another room and they took me into a room by myself. It was dimly lighted and this sort of soft amber light came from over head. The room was dome-shaped with a bulkhead ribbing effect. The men still had their hats on and I could just make out their faces. They looked human but they were odd-looking. They had elongated features and slightly larger eyes. They laid me down on this table. I sensed what was coming next but the next thing I knew, we were back in the car driving down the same road. It was quiet in the car. No one spoke until we arrived at our destination, a store in another town near Burney. The town was dark and the store closed. Grandmother was confused because the store should have been open. She checked the time and realized it was midnight. I remember her being quite perplexed about it. She just couldn't understand how she made such an error. We had missing time. Later in my life I would know of this well, from hundreds of other accounts. This all happened before I had read "The Interrupted Journey".

There were other strange moments in my many stays at the Burney house. There was an abandoned barn across from us out in an open field. The house we lived in was a log cabin and, at one time, the main office for the logging business. The barn was used to service the big trucks that hauled the logs. There was an old truck there long-rusted and rotting away. The barn was huge and inside was more abandoned truck parts and old equipment. It was all kind of creepy and I would look over at it, sitting on the porch in the early evening, with both fascination and wonder.

On some nights, I got out of bed and would sneak out to go into that barn. And like the plateau at my home in Pacifica, there were beings there too. I was in some sort of school there and I wish I could remember more about it. But somehow I still remember the lessons.

The last time I stayed in Burney was in 1963. I was 11 years old. I spent the entire year there. And I remember very well that November, where I was. Walking home from school, I arrived to the terrible news that President Kennedy had been assassinated. I really loved Kennedy for so many reasons. I admired his service in WW2 on PT 109 for one, and mostly because he was sending us to the Moon. I was devastated. I went home for Christmas and never went back to Burney.

I checked Google Earth in order to find the old house and to look at Burney to see how well my memory serves me; still and couldn't find the house. Everything was about the same. The town didn't grow much over the years. When I followed the roads and trails I knew from my time there, I found where the house had been. It was like looking at an archaeological site. You could see where the house was and the old lumber yard from so long ago. Either a fire burned it all down or it was just abandoned and torn down over time. I recognized the road and the rocks that line the roadway leading to the house. I could see where the barn was and beyond that the huge ancient lava flow I used to hike in.

Chapter Ten
Losing My Dad

It was the summer of 1964. Mom was staying in Korea for the summer. She loved it there and always wanted to live there. Aunt Hazel was staying with me for the summer. Dad would pick me up on weekends and we'd build models, race slot cars and go to the races. We were starting to get closer than we had ever been.

Dad lived with his second wife, Jean, in a beautiful home in Terra Linda in Marin County. He had just been made vice-president of the engineering company. The firm worked on government contracts for the Navy, primarily on our nuclear submarines; another interest we shared. He worked on the Skipjack and the Washington, our first boomer. I was so proud of him. He was living the great life in style. I loved being there. There were great parties there on the weekends. Outside would be all my favorite cars from Porsche to Ferrari lined up and down the block. His friends were all professionals, doctors, engineers, scientists and even famous racecar drivers.

He had a big slot car track in the back and would often have his racing buddies over to race 1/32 Indy cars and even bet on the race. It was just a great place to be for a kid. I still have, to this day, a large scenic slot car track I play on in our home.

The last time I saw Dad was in the morning before he went to work in Mare Island. I remember it like it was yesterday. He gave me a kiss and a hug and, as he walked out the door, he paused. He gave me this look and said he would see me soon. Jean drove me home in her Mercedes that Monday. It was summer and I didn't have to be in school. Later that day, I was playing in the garage with the slot car track Dad had given me when Aunt Hazel walked in and asked me outside. I got out to the front and she asked me to sit down on the retainer wall to the driveway. I knew something was wrong. I could see the look on her face. She told me that Dad had been killed on the way to work. He was driving in the fog on the way to Mare Island when a drunk driver forced him off the road head-on and off a bridge. The fog was so low to the ground that morning; Dad couldn't see that he would go off the road and into the ravine. The world stopped for me. I was forever changed.

My Dad's killer was let go. He didn't have a criminal record, had a family and a good job. He had never been in trouble before and pleaded mercy on the court. He went free. This put quite a chip on my shoulder to say the least. From my perspective, the system had let me down and I became a rebel. Not to mention President Kennedy being assassinated only a few months before.

My mantra became: question authority, question everything; resist. I am still the rebel. This all happened just in time for the Sixties, the revolution and

Vietnam. The Beatles were just about to hit the scene. Like today, it was crazy times and I was starting to discover girls, rock & roll, and cars, especially sports cars.

I met my friend Mike in 6th grade, a kindred spirit. We both loved guitars, rock and roll, science fiction and more. Mike came along at a good time in my life. I needed a friend with whom I could relate. I remember even at that very young age he was a member of MENSA. He would read a book a day. He was a genius and a pal. But I never told Mike about my experiences.

By my 14th birthday we had met my friend Chris. Chris, Mike and I were great friends. We even formed a rock band.

Chapter Eleven

Moving Again

By the end of my 14th year, Mom bought a house up in the hills overlooking Sharps Park. It over-looked the coast and, from there, I could see the curvature of the earth on the ocean's horizon. I could watch ships come and go. I could see Pedro Point and more.

The next year I started high school. I was not doing well in school; I didn't like it to be truthful. All I wanted to do was be creative and study science and art. Playing in the band really helped. We played at school dances and shared lots of time together listening to the greats and playing our own music.

I was fortunate to have an incredible science teacher. I used to stay after school all the time to talk about astrophysics and astronomy. Mike stayed too. We loved the guy. Mr. Wheary was his name. He had a great passion for photography and telescopes. He loved teaching us all he could. My other teacher in school that I loved dearly was a great lady and photographer. Anne Sweeney. She had a great photo lab at our high school where she taught me to shoot, develop my own film, and print my photos. Both teachers imparted on me many great philosophies that I still live by today. All and all it was good.

Things were quiet and although I continued to watch the skies; I was watching girls and rock bands more. I watched the space race too. I was grateful to Mom who allowed me to miss school to watch every mission I could. I still thought then about being an astronaut or astronomer. I remember well the very first moment Neil Armstrong set foot on the Moon and said those now famous words. I ran outside the house expecting the town to be going wild. Instead I walked outside to hear silence. I started cheering and hooting and hollering. "We landed on the Moon!!!! And a man came out of his house and told me to shut up. The bumps in the night seemed to pass for a while. It was quiet again, for now.

Chapter Twelve
It Starts Again

Mom had a piano in the house and at night, after I went to bed, she would play before she went to sleep. I always enjoyed her playing. She would play everything from Debussy to Beethoven. Moon Light Sonata was a favorite and Clair de Lune was another. One night while I was lying in bed listening, a tingling feeling came over me. I felt dreamy and as I looked towards the window at the foot of my bed I saw the lights again.

They came through the window and ran along the foot of the bed until they touched me. Then I saw them; shadows of forms backlit by the lights. They were floating in the air coming straight for me. To my surprise, they came through the window like ghosts; I began to float from my bed. They pulled me a long and I passed right through the window with them. I could feel a slight tug on my body as we passed through the glass, an odd feeling. Mom's music faded and the silence of the night fell upon me. It was deathly silent. As we rose into the air, I could see the black disc shape in the sky and, as before, a doorway opened and soft yellow amber light comes from behind it. I wasn't afraid, I was glad they had come back. Somehow I felt safe and cared for, as if their world was mine (I would later learn it is). I longed to be there. It all felt so soft, even loving. We passed through the door and inside were this immense interior of arched hallways and doorways. They took me to a room that was softly lighted in a pale white yellow light. There was, what looked like, shear curtains hanging in a circle around a round bed of sorts on the floor. It was round. She was waiting for me. I say her because this was a woman with whom I fell in love. She had long golden blond hair and was wearing white. Her face was beautiful but she didn't look like any human being I had ever seen. So striking were her features, overly enlarged eyes. They were green and her irises wide and dark pupils. Her cheekbones were high and chin pointed and elongated. Her lips were thin and her body fine-boned. She was beautiful and called to me to lie down with her. I saw the smaller beings stood watching in the shadows of the room. First we talked intimately at length about my interests in the universe. She told me many things about it, that there are many civilizations and worlds. She said we all shared in our ancestry with them, that the same DNA and life's building blocks had been spread far and wide across the galaxy long ago. She told me of Mars. That once it was a thriving civilization there and that humans had escaped during the Martian world's demise. Our civilization no longer remembers their past. In fact, even worse, we had nearly completely separated ourselves from the reality of the Cosmos and this was a path that would not end well for us, if we didn't change and embrace that which we really are, and move into the stars. We are all born of the stars; yet we seldom look towards them. Instead we make war among ourselves over greed and lust. It was hinted at that this same thing happen on Mars.

This same message was and will be repeated throughout my life experience. She, like Mr. Lee, told me so many things I still hold true and dear to-day. I'll never know for sure if any of what she told me was true, however one thing was, that we need to unit as one race and explore the stars. This too has been a common theme in my life.

I felt like I knew her and had all my life. She told me I lived before and we have always known each other. That she had found me again. Something I must have practiced in the past kept my soul, my identity, intact. Then she started holding me closer and closer. Her touch was warm and seemed to penetrate deep into my heart and soul. We lay down. She removed my cloths and made love to me. It was beautiful and forever bonding. I was spellbound, but when it was all over they took me away and back to my room. They told me I wouldn't remember and I feel back asleep.

When I awoke the next day, I had this longing for her. A sadness that I had lost someone I loved. I thought about her all the day in school and in time it passed. Clearly I didn't forget. I thought of her only as a dream. But deep inside as always I knew there was more to it. Clearly I didn't forget and over the months to come, she visited me again and again.

Over the next two years things slowly quieted again. I went to school and lived the life of a teen-ager. In time, I began to forget but never complete-ly.

Chapter Thirteen
Start Trek and 2001

At Sixteen I had discovered and fell in love with Star Trek. I loved Star Trek for many reasons. With what I had experienced, it was not surprising: one race, united and exploring the universe. That was Gene Roddenberry's message and it was one I already shared.

I was still in my band with my best friends Mike and Chris and, one day, Mike told me that he had just seen a movie he thought was better than Star Trek. It was called, "2001: A Space Odyssey". He couldn't really explain it to me and that it would just be better if I went and saw it. He told me it was the best space movie he had ever seen.

That was all it took for me. The next weekend I got on a bus and went into San Francisco. I went to the Golden Gate Theater. It had the movie in 70mm and Cinerama. I had never heard of Stanley Kubrick or seen any of his films. I knew who Author C. Clarke was, as I was a reader of science fiction. I had no idea what I was in for. I sat there in front of the huge curtains covering the screen while music of György Ligeti played. It was haunting, eerie and created an atmosphere that sent chills through me. In fact, the piece that played was entitled "Atmospheres". I knew then I was in for something totally different than anything I would experience in a movie. As I would soon learn, it wasn't a movie but an experience, a wakeup call of enormous proportions.

The lights went down slowly and music faded. The MGM Lion graphic was projected on unopened curtains. There was a low rumble and the curtains opened slowly. Once they cleared the enormous curved screen, the Lion fades, and I saw this huge shadow of the moon in space moving downward. The music, "Also Sprach Zarathustra" played and, as it did, the moon revealed the Earth and the sun rising over it. The music built to such an intensity tears ran down my face. I'd come home!

On the way home I was in a daze. My mind kept cycling through what I had just experienced. From my point of view, this was more than a movie and there was something about the monolith that called to me. It all made sense and felt right. This was more than science fiction but maybe a channeled memory of something that really happened. I could not stop thinking of this movie for days afterwards I went back and saw it every weekend I could, over and over again. It was calling to me. I wanted to learn all I could about the filmmaker and the writer. I learned all I could about Kubrick and started watching his other films.

This was a pivotal time in my life. I was 16 years old. I had to make a decision about my life's direction. What did I want to do with my life? It was clear to me filmmaking was the one thing I could do that combined everything I loved into one medium. Filmmaking had the power to change people's lives and change the future. Science fiction has changed the future or better, set the future we live now. Everything from a trip to the Moon to our cell phones and tablets come from it.

I wanted in. I read "The Making of 2001" and "Stanley Kubrick Directs". I remember Kubrick writing that the best film school you could ever have was to go out and make a movie. So I found Mom's old 8mm camera, bought some film and made movies.

First thing I did was to build a Gemini space capsule, get Matt Masterman, build some space backdrop and, using stop motion, made my first space movie. I later bought a Fairchild 8mm camera with sounds and I made some science fiction movies with my friends. All I could think about was making films and writing scripts and shooting them. I read everything I could about Kubrick. I studied all his films I could. I did this all through high school. When I graduated in 1970, I swore to my classmates I'd go to Hollywood and make movies. I did just that.

Chapter Fourteen
My Career in the Movies

I lived at home while I attended college. I read in the San Francisco Chronicle a story about a film studio called the American Zoetrope in San Francisco. The article was about George Lucas, of whom I first became aware from his work I saw on QUED PBS on TV. It was called, "THX11384eb" and was his final for film school. That movie captivated me and influenced some of my early short films. In this article they wrote about his making a feature film version of his short film called, "THX1138". The article went on talking about the studio's owner, Francis Ford Coppola. What really caught my attention about the article was the fact they wanted to help young filmmakers. Well, that was enough for me. I boldly called them and introduced myself as the young filmmaker they wanted to help. To my surprise I was invited to visit them. I was so excited I couldn't stand it. At American Zoetrope I met Bart Patton, then Francis and George Lucas. We went to Francis's office and he pulled down his big screen and asked me to show him my films. So I screened two of my films in 8mm with sound on his big screen. I was nervous and scared to death but I did it.

That was the beginning of a wonderful time in my life surrounded by such amazing filmmakers. Later I made a 16 mm film called "Arthur" and they let me using their 3-picture Kem editing bay and more. I learned the craft of filmmaking and helped around their studio in exchange. I was following closely Kubrick's teaching. Go out and make a movie.

Francis was so nice. He even drove me to the bus station when my Alfa Romeo broke down. They took me to parties in Marin County and concerts at the Filmore Auditorium. One day there I was editing, an English voice I knew spoke to me from behind. I turned around and standing there was Arthur C Clarke, in the doorway with his briefcase in hand. On the briefcase was the Apollo 11 patch. He was dressed in a suit and tie like he had just walked off the set of "2001". He asked me if I knew where Francis was? This was one of those Forest Gump moments (as that later in life my love Mary would call it, the Forest Gump Syndrome) that would continue through my life. He was there to talk about "Childhoods End" that was being considered for a feature film. Francis and Kubrick were talking. I'll never forget the letter from Stanley he posted on the bulletin board outside his office for all of us to see. I would look at the letter and just be awe-struck. Unfortunately the film was never made and I was lucky to meet Arthur.

I worked there for a while and later I started another film. I needed the studio's help once again. I had to talk to Francis about it and he was on the set of "The Conversation". So he invited me down town to the location where they were shooting and I had lunch with him. I met Gene Hackman. Little did I know at the time I would meet him again a few years later when I was working with Oliver Reed on a feature film. I told Francis about my new film and he listened. He was always kind to me. But when I asked to use studio equipment once again he said no. He was very nice about it and explained that too many people at the studio had taken advantage of him and abused the privilege even taken equipment and not returning it. He pointed out that I had never done any of these things and we had no problems, but if he allowed me to use the studio again for free he would have to allow everyone. Soon after that conversation, I stopped going to the Zoetrope. Things changed and Francis had left for LA.

Without help, I couldn't make another film so I went back to community college and took media and art classes. In my art class, I met a man there who was painting a science fiction painting like I was, but his was different. We talked and eventually took a trip to his home. There he had all kinds of interesting sculptures and artwork he had done that were based on the Famous monsters and Science Fiction films I loved. He made his own masks, life cast and even forms of prosthetic make-ups. I was fascinated and thought that I might want to learn this craft. One of my favorite movies was "Planet of the Apes" and I wanted so badly to learn how that was done. Now I could. Doug helped me make my first life mask and I sculpted my first ape face based on pictures from the movie. Later, I did it again and again perfecting it and made very accurate renditions of Roddy McDowall's prosthetic make-up.

I was invited to attend a science fiction convention at the St. Francis Hotel in San Francisco. There I met a man named Ricky Schwartz. We talked all night and he invited me up to his room where he showed me real prosthetic appliances he had from "Planet of the Apes". I showed him my work and he told me, if I really wanted to succeed at this, I needed to come to LA. He was right.

I stayed in Pacifica a short while longer and, thanks to my friend Mike, I used his garage as a lab and sculpted all kinds of creatures and perfected the Apes make-up and costume. It got me work at Halloween around town because people found out about me and I started making money. I would later go to conventions in make-up and sell ape appliances and foam latex Vulcan ears. This would lead to my meeting all kinds of people at these Conventions, such as Gene Roddenberry, Ray Bradbury, George Clayton Johnson, and so many others.

It was around 1973 when I left Pacifica with my girlfriend Marlin and moved to LA. We got a studio apartment on Doheny Blvd. and I started my career.

I first met Rick Baker by surfing the phone book. I eventually found the right number and I was invited to his home. I interned with Joe Balasco. I was invited to work on the "Planet of the Apes" TV shows for few days. It was an amazing time because there I met Roddy and John Chambers, the man that created the make-ups for the movies. My career just continued to unfold and I got more and more work in

Hollywood. This kept me in the film industry and in money. It was my hope to write a script, and using the resources I now had, make a film.

It was about this time I met Ve Neill although that wasn't her name when I met her. We started dating and it wasn't too long before I found out she loved doing make-up. She was fascinated by my work and wanted to take her own great talent to the next level and work in the industry. We were a great team. I'd make the prosthetic appliances and she would apply them.

We eventually moved in together and got a place in Toluca Lake only a mile or so from Rick Bakers house. I spent a lot of time with Rick and through his mentorship; I was able to get better shows. Eventually, as his popularity rose, he started referring jobs to me. Ve and I did a number of B pictures together and had a really good time doing them. "Laser Blast" was one. It was my first job for Charlie Band and that eventually led to my writing and producing my first motion picture. The project was bought on two pages entitled, "Vortex" which later became, "The Day Time Ended".

These were stressful, trying times for our relationship. Ve was always on location because her career was taking off. I was all caught up in my film.

The last picture we worked on together was "Star Trek the Motion Picture." Fred Philips hired me on to the film to do Nimoy's ears, another one of those Forest Gump moments. Something that was a dream in high school was coming true and I was on top of the world. I got Ve involved working on the show too where she did her first union picture after just getting into Local 706, the make-up artist and hairstyles union chapter of IATSE.

Meanwhile, I had built an observatory on our roof with a large refractor telescope inside. I would go up there at night and just watch the sky. I started reading books again on the subject. I started spending a lot of time with the study of UFOs and talking about it. Shortly after getting into the Union Ve wanted to move on. We separated. However, we have always stayed friends. One of the main reasons she wanted to leave me was my obsession with UFOs. You see, the year "Close Encounters of a Third Kind" was released the film awoke something in me. "The Day Time Ended" was very influenced by that film. The sleeping experience that I had stowed away had been released. For Ve it was too much. One day on the way to see "Jaws" she told me she wanted to talk, the talk. I was very broken hearten about it but I understood. She was kind about it and it was a peaceful break-up.

I moved back to Toluca Lake and rented an apartment by myself. It was so hard being alone. For me this was the first time since I went to college and met Marlin. It was pretty lonely so started starting going out and made new friends. I had girl friends and things were better. But at first it was pretty hard. Although the work kept coming I was pretty unhappy. I missed Ve. But this is about the time when things started getting strange again.

Chapter Fifteen

Strange Days and Nights

During my time in Toluca Lake at the apartment I spent a lot of time out at night. I was young, in my twenties and had money and a nice sports car. I dated a lot but never really found anyone with whom I wanted to have a relationship. I didn't want a relationship; I was out to have fun. Often I had friends over and lots of girls. We'd go out on the town all night and party hard.

One night Ricky Schwartz came over and brought and couple of girls he knew. I was still getting ready and was in my bedroom when I heard a thought in my mind. "Go to the window and you'll see something". So I went to the window and parted the blinds. Looking out I saw a disc-shaped object glowing an amber color. I knew right away by its strange movement that it wasn't a plane. Additionally, it was lacking NAV lights and anti- collision lights. The first thing that went through my mind was Ricky and the girls. Witnesses! I went into the front room and took them to the kitchen where there was a better view. I pointed it out to them and they watched it with great interest. I told them to stay there and watch it. I wanted to go outside and see it. I could not hear anything. I ran down the stairs and outside and it was gone. I ran back up and found them standing in the kitchen in a daze. I asked what happened and they said it burst into two objects, got really bright and shot straight up and out of site. They were in shock and the girls were very scared. I was surprised that they were so disturbed by the event, but they were. The rest of the night at dinner and out on the town it was all they talked about. I got back to the apartment alone around 2:00 a.m. What happened next was amazing.

I couldn't get the event off my mind. The lights were off in the apartment and I was in a solemn mood. I went into the kitchen and looked out the window towards where we had seen the object. The courtyard below was dark. Past a certain hour at night they turned off. The sky was dark and I could see a few stars. Suddenly the sky burst bright blue white. For a moment it was brighter than daylight. It faded and stopped. It was at that moment in the darkness that my kitchen lights came on and flickered. All the courtyard lights did too. Yet they were turned off, all the lights that lighted up where florescent lights. I know what a Tesla coil could do to those florescent tubes when they were placed near them. They would light up. This had to be the same effect and which meant that, just at that moment, an enormous amount of static energy had been released, or AC high voltage, either way it was huge and a Tesla big enough to do that was unlikely. I knew it had something to do with the object that we saw that night. For months to come I would see these flashes on cloudless nights around the San Fernando Valley. I also saw plenty of UFOs too. It was a hot bed period.

I had two girlfriends I knew well that would come over and we'd spend hours talking about things like UFOs. As always, they were skeptical and I always encouraged good skepticism, to never take my word for it or anyone else. This is how you come to know things rather than having beliefs. I don't want to believe, I want to know.

One evening just after sunset I was alone and watching TV and there was this loud banging on my door. It was Ronda and her friend. They looked exasperated. They were frantic to tell me about something they just saw. They had been driving my way in Toluca Lake when they saw this dark disc-shaped object in the sky. It was low and hovering over the homes in a residential part of Toluca Lake. They followed it as it moved slowly through the neighborhood. At one point, they saw people in their front yards. One was watering the lawn. They stopped the car and got out. The object was barely moving. They wanted a better look. They saw the man watering the yard and got his attention. They told him to look at the object. He acted uninterested and hardly reacted to it except to say, "Oh yeah. Look at that" and just went about watering the yard. By now the two girls were quite frustrated. They saw kids in the street playing ball. They tried to get them to look at it and again very little reaction. They just ignored it. This kept happening and people just refused to take notice or worse would say they don't see anything at all. Ronda and her friend got back into the car and followed the object. Eventually it came over my apartment, stopped and disappeared. This is when they came to me. I was told point blank that they never wanted to see such a thing. It frightened them and I'm the one that should have seen it. "Why us" they asked? When they left, we never talked about it again.

Through my experience with these events I would come to know this lack of reaction or memory of seeing a UFO. And in this field of interest it is most common and frustrating. Events like this continue to occur. UFOs were reported by my friends to be seen near where I lived very often. My friend Jim came to me one night and told me of being in a restaurant. The power started flickering on and off. Car alarms were going off in the parking lot out-front. He went out there to check his car only to find a group of people standing in the lot looking up at this disc hovering over them. He was excited and was thrilled with the event but he was the exception to the norm.

I eventually left the Toluca Lake in 1978 and moved to a house in Burbank in the foothills where still more strange events were in my future.

Chapter Sixteen

Messages from the Other Side

I continued to date and see girlfriends. I never found anyone I wanted to be with more than a nice date and some good times. I was only in my mid-twenties, restless and searching. I worked on films and TV shows of all kinds. This filled much of my time.

I went to a party one night and I met Judy. She was this beautiful sweet girl and we fell in love. She was married but separated from her husband. Later on she moved in with me and it was wonderful. I worked hard and so did she. It was wonderful to have her there to come home to after all the hard work shooting movies and doing creature effects. Often, I would talk to her about the things I had experienced. She knew of my interest about UFO's and humored me about it. She really didn't think much of life after death, near-death experiences or UFO's, ghost, or beings from other worlds. But she was never bothered by it all and didn't give me a bad time about it in anyway. She just had such a good heart. We had a lot of good times together but, in time, I started to change how I felt about her. I was working closely with Oliver Reed on a movie. I was there so many long days and nights and he and I went out every night to party in the city. The make-up artist on the show that did all the straight make-up, while I did Oliver's Mr. Hyde make-up was someone I had my eye on. Karen was this talented, beautiful woman with whom I was working closely and I started to have feelings for her. We both were make-up artists and loved filmmaking. We had more in common with each other than Judy and I. Karen and I were close but still had feelings for Judy. I made some poor choices. I asked Judy to get her own place and move out. I had decided Judy wasn't the one. I wanted to be able to date again and live alone. It was too soon in my young life to get serious after having one serious relationship after the other. Before Ve, I was with Marlin (whom I met in college), but we had different interests too and when I met Ve for the same reasons, we were better matched for our common ground interest in make-up effects and film.

I was out with Karen one night at dinner. We had a nice evening and returned back to the Burbank house for a nightcap. I checked my phone machine for messages, as I always did, and found one from Judy just checking on me and saying she missed me. I figured I'd call her back the next day and spent some time with Karen. Later she went home. I had to get up early the next day for a screening of a Roger Corman movie I had just worked on. I went to bed that night without giving it a further thought. I was tired and excited about the screening because, for a Roger Corman movie, it was a pretty big deal with an all-star cast and many creatures and aliens I had made for "Battle Beyond the Stars". That morning I had this vivid dream about Judy. It had to be around 6:00 am when I had the dream, because I woke up from the dream around that time.

The dream was as follows: I felt weightless and floating in a realm I can only describe as spherical. The outer edges of the sphere were clouds and soft sort of pastel colors glowing within and changing much as a RGB LED would today. I could hear an ambient music in the background. It was at this point I saw Judy. It was like a new age cliché. She was naked with only wearing panties; she was moving toward me and wrapped her arms around me. We turned slowly while embracing. She kissed me and told me she loved me. She said it was time for her to move on. She said not to worry; she was happy, so very happy. She kept saying this is great. I feel so good. She told me I had been right about dying. That we do continue on and there is life on the other side. She also said I was right about the aliens. She called them that. I was never sure but I found it funny she would tell me these things. She said she wasn't in pain and that I shouldn't be sad. She just wanted to tell me these things and to have a last moment together. While writing about this now, my emotions are still so strong about that moment. I felt such love from her and I felt sad anyway. I didn't want to lose her. But she told me I never could. She understood something then I only now grasp years later. But she let go of me and floated back; disappearing into the clouds and was gone. I woke up and thought to myself that was a pretty strange dream. I was so much in a hurry to get ready for the screening I swept it aside for the moment.

I got up, got dressed and drove down to the theater for the screening. Everyone had a great time and enjoyed the movie. It was a wonderful day. On the way home I thought about the dream. What the heck was that all about? I had no idea. But when I got home and checked the messages, I heard her call from the night before and wanted to call her. What stopped me dead in my tracks was the next message. It was her girlfriend. Judy had died during the night on a friend's sofa. They figured the time of death was around 6:00 a.m. She was found only wearing panties. What are the odds of this being a coincidence? In the billions, I figured. I was devastated. I can't begin to explain the feelings and pain I experienced at that moment and for the weeks to come. I knew then that I did not have a dream. What I experienced was real and took a great effort from Judy to do. I will be forever in her debt for such a gift as she gave to me.

Mom had the very similar experience when she was a child. One night she woke up to her grandmother sitting on her bed with her. She told her how much she loved her but it was time for her to go. Then my mom woke up, startled out of her sleep by the phone ringing. Her mother, my grandmother answered the phone. There was a long silence and then my grandmother started crying. Her mother had just died. It would seem that this ability just runs in my family on both sides. Later on I would realize this had something to do with my experiences with UFOs and visitors. This whole experience was one. Not separate but deeply connected.

Chapter Seventeen

Gilly

For many long weeks after Judy passed, I suffered physical illness and grief. It felt like food poisoning but I had not eaten anything that would have caused it. I stayed with Karen who took care of me for a couple of weeks, until I recovered. I returned home to the dark and silent house. I was ready to move on somewhere different and escape that past. I have always been one to move on and not dwell in the past. I had to get working and move on. Nothing I could do would change the past. Again I started going out and dating. I worked hard on the contracts I was still getting.

I was invited to a long time friend's house for a party. There were many people I knew there; one I had noticed off and on at those parties for a long time. But she always had a date or boy friend, so I just admired her from afar. At this party she was alone. She was this beautiful English girl with long blond hair that extended beyond her waist. You could pick her out of a crowd in a glance. I finally got up the nerve to talk to her that night. I told her what I had just been through. My stomach was still bothering me even though I was much better. We talked most of the night and then I went home. As I was just getting in bed the phone rang. It was Gilly. She asked me how my tummy was feeling and I told her about the same. We talked for some time and I went to sleep. Next day we talked again and we made a date. I'll never forget her driving over to the Burbank house dressed like a little hippie girl and driving and 61 VW bug with a peace sign on it. She brought me a chicken dinner and we had a wonderful night. Later she took me in the bug over to her house in Silver Lake. An old home from the Hollywood days nestled into the heavy growth of the hillside. We continued to date and one day she asked me to move in. I did and I never looked back. I continued to work on films for Larry Cohen, Roger Corman, and others. We had a great time living together with her young daughter Beth.

Again although we shared so many of the same interests there were many we didn't have together. As my relationships before Gilly, the interests we didn't share would take their toll on both of us.

We both loved so many of the same movies and watched films all the time. She loved working with me on the movies and TV shows. "Close Encounters" was one of our favorites. But for Gilly, this wasn't happening to me. Not in our life. But she was starting to see that I was a bit like the character Neary in "Close Encounters". But for now, she would look the other way.

Chapter Eighteen

They're Back Again

It wasn't long after my meeting and moving in with Gilly that the visitors came back. I remember clearly one night waking up to an orange glow in the window and I could not move. I could see people, tall and thin standing around the bed watching. Just staring at us. I couldn't make their faces out but only these elongated human forms.   I feel back asleep struggling to stay awake and then it was morning. Gilly told me that morning that she had a strange dream about an orange ball in the window and men in the room with us. Thought it was odd but didn't mention it again. This caught my attention. I hadn't really talked to her much about my interests in UFOs but in time I would. She always thought that there might well be UFOs from other worlds but that was about as far as she went with the subject. We watched "Close Encounters" together more than once. It was always a bit emotional for me but for her too but for different reasons. I related it to it deeply and couldn't understand how. She longed for something to happen for the planet that would bring about positive change. It wasn't until I showed her "The UFO Incident" that things started to become alarming for me. "The UFO Incident" was based on Barney and Betty Hill's abduction in the early sixties, a widely known case and one of the first of its kind. It was based on their book the "Interrupted Journey".

Universal Studios did a fantastic job of doing the TV movie just as the book. This is rarely done. We watched it together. Everything was fine until we got to the hypnosis session with Barney and Betty. I could not control my emotions. I started crying and I was embarrassed and so unsettled I left the room. She couldn't understand what was wrong. I couldn't either at the time, but it so moved me I found it hard to watch. And I still do. What had just happened to me? I wouldn't know for a long time, but often Gilly liked to show the film to friends when they'd come over for dinner. I would try to avoid watching it with them and this bothered her. She'd ask, "What's wrong?" And she'd become annoyed telling me to snap out of it because we had company. This was the beginning of a turmoil that would become part of our relationship and not a good one. So much was ahead of us and it had just begun. We didn't live very long at her place in Silverlake when we moved to a house in Glendale. I needed the space and a good garage setup for my work. The place we found had a big garage and an enclosed courtyard that made the perfect studio.

Things were good and work was flowing in. I was working on a lot of film projects and TV commercials, "A-Team," "Ghost Busters", "Fright Night" and "The Stuff", to name a few. My gorilla suit work was growing all the time. I did all kinds of TV commercials, movies and TV shows with my realistic gorilla suits. I made the suits and did the acting. Things were good. Rick Stratton, Mark Siegel and I worked together all the time. We are all good friends to this day and I would always involve them in any project I did and they would do the same for me. Mark and I often went on astronomy star parties with our telescopes. Mt. Wilson was one sight but the best one was on Mt. Pino, high up on the mountain and far away from the city lights.

On one such occasion we stayed his actor friend Tony Plana's cabin in Fraser Park. This is also at Mt. Pino and there was a large clearing in the trees, not far from his Toni's cabin. We took both our Celestrons to this field. It was a great night with great seeing conditions. A slight breeze and the night sounds, it was a perfect evening. We looked at all kinds of objects and one in particular I wanted to do a long-term tracked time exposure of was the Ring Nebula. In those days, around the mid-eighties we had SLR cameras and film. And the only way to get a picture, with all the color of the nebula, was to track the object by hand and slowly over 20-40 minutes expose it on film. This required a great deal of patience and concentration.

I was about 20 minutes into my exposure when I noticed a bright light being shined at me from the right. This annoyed me and I couldn't believe Mark of all people would be so careless as to be using such a flashlight. If you use any kind of light at all, it should be colored red as to not dilate your eyes and maintain good night vision. Not to mention it could be very bad for the exposure. It continued and I finally took my eyes away from the eyepiece and looked towards Mark. He was just standing there

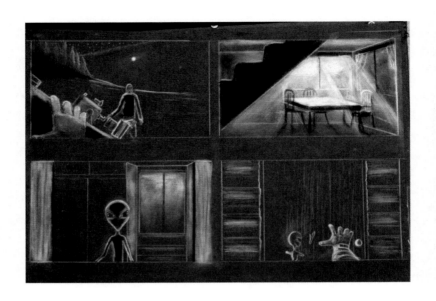

with his back to me looking at this large round softly glowing sphere. It was a soft amber color and seems to pulsate very slowly.

(Here are some of the Storyboards I drew for Yvonne as requested after our session. The additional images in the board show some of the things that happened later that night at the cabin.)

I said to Mark, "Mark do you see that?" he said yes. I replied back, "good".

The object got quite close to us. This is when I noticed the vacuum. That is to say all of the night sounds were gone and we were in complete silence. I decided to walk over to get a closer look. Mark was frightened for me and said I shouldn't do that. But I did anyway. I wasn't afraid. I wanted a closer look but as I did it backed away from me

more and more until it took off to the right and quickly moved over the field dropping over a ridge. As I
got to the ridge I stopped. It descended to the valley
below where I watched it descend to the valley floor,
cut across it into the distance to where I could no
longer see it. It was at this moment I noticed that the
night sounds and slight breeze returned. In retrospect, it seemed that time stood still during the
event.

That evening we returned to the cabin to spend
the night. I woke up the next day and we drove back
to Glendale. I felt a bit hung over the next day and
on the way home thought about the night and what
we had seen. I wasn't aware at the time that more
happened at the cabin, but in a few years to come I
would.

Once I got to the house, Gilly greeted us and we
sat around and talked about the UFO. Mark seemed
reluctant to talk about the incident. But he did and
Gilly remembered his doing so even though a few
weeks later he had no memory of the entire event
while Gilly still did. As I have said before, this is not
at all uncommon. It happens all the time, the fact
that Gilly did remember his talking about it confirms
my memory of the event.

Years later, Mark moved to Sausalito, California.
He called me one night and told me he had been
having nightmares about a UFO outside his windows shining lights inside his apartment. I recently
asked Mark about the nightmares and he has no

memory of them or his telling me. Sometimes when you do have witnesses they will soon forget what they saw leading people that this happens to question their own sanity.

Gilly and I lived at the Glendale house until 1986 then we moved less than a mile away to a new house. It was there our Creatures Effects Company grew even more. We had a huge yard and built large storage sheds and used them to work in. We had a crew of people and friends working for us. We had more projects than we could keep up with and things were good.

Halley's Comet was to be in the night skies again and the Celestron was out showing friends and neighbors the comet.

We started a new character for a McDonald's commercial called Mac Tonight, a singing crescent moon man. I got my first cell phone. I discovered the radio controlled model airplane. However, something was looming on the horizon that would not only rock my world but millions of other people's too.

In 1986 Gilly became very ill. A uterine tumor had become very enlarged and burst nearly killing her. We weren't married and she didn't have health insurance. On the other hand, I did. I was covered by my Screen Actors Guild heath coverage. So after she got out of the hospital, and many expensive doctor bills later that we paid, we decided to get

married so she could have my health care coverage.

She was still recovering and a week later I had a
friend of ours, a minister with the Universal Life
Church, marry us at our home in Glendale. Gilly
went on to join the Screen Actors Guild and worked
happily puppeteering for Mac Tonight other creatures and my gorilla suit. We both made lots of
money from the residuals we received from the
work. They were happy times.

Chapter Nineteen:

Communion

I don't recall exactly when, sometime in1987, I was watching a talk show and this man was talking about having contact experiences with what he called, "the Visitors". As I watched the show, he presented his book, "Communion" and when they showed the book on the screen there was a face staring at me I knew, but how? He talked about the UFOs he had seen and the strange events written about in his, now famous, book. I was fascinated. I watched him as he appeared on many different shows on television over that year. His book became a best seller with over 10 million copies sold. This book was changing the world and it was about to change mine. He had become a household name and I asked Gilly to get the book for me. I just had to read it. One day she brought it home. That night, after a long day at work, I stayed up quite late reading the book. Every page I turned I felt this familiarity that I couldn't explain. I related to it deeply. I could not put it down. Even now I can still feel the excitement. Like the "UFO Incident", it moved my emotions deeply. I started to think about my own experiences as I read it. Flash backs to all those things I experienced up to this point. It was powerful, moving. I came to the realization that this same experience, whatever it is, is happening to me, and it had been since I was a child. The next day in the morning the crew was showing up for work. Gilly made me tea and I sat there observing everything around me differently than I had the day before. My world had just changed for better or worse. I had to know more. Once I finished the book I wanted so badly to meet Whitley, share with him the things I experienced. To tell him he wasn't alone. But he would soon know this anyway. He wasn't. But it wasn't long after that more and more people that had experiences the same phenomenon were coming forward at breakneck speed. Whitley got thousands of letters that would later become the "Communion Letters".

I studied a great deal about this experience. I read everything I could, I watched all the shows and interviews I could about close encounter witnesses. I didn't know what to do so I kept it all to myself, as I had in the past, however with a different awareness than I had before. I continued to work in motion pictures while keeping a keen eye to Whitley's and others' progress.

In 1988 we moved again to a nice house up in Granada Hills, a suburb on the edge of the San Fernando Valley. I setup up shop there and continued my motion picture creature work. Here and there I started to do art about UFOs and even sculptures of the visitors. During this time things seemed quiet, however unknown to me, I was having interactions that I didn't remember. I was constantly having disturbing dreams and waking up with cuts, bruises, and strange triangular markings on my body; and I had no recall of how I received them. I started paying closer attention to this. Mainly keeping track of my injuries during work and making note of them, especially before I went to bed. If they did have a more terrestrial source, it was happening while I was asleep.

From 1988 until 1991, I kept my eye to what was happening to me and in the news of this field. I learned more and more about the key players in the quest to learn more about what they called, "Alien Abduction". Which was a term with which I never felt comfortable. Simply because I felt it was pure conjecture to surmise that we were dealing with something from another planet. I didn't know that. Neither did anyone else although they would claim these things based on their theories, and not factual collected data. It leaned well to the skeptics and the media's posture that anyone claiming these things was not in their right mind. Again, I don't want to believe, I want to know. All during this period, I kept watching the skies. I saw so many UFOs I lost count. The activity continues and it was getting harder and harder to remain silent.

I learned of Bud Hopkins work with abductees, as they were called. And how hypnosis helped recovered block memories. I considered, maybe if I could have this done, I might find out if I was just imagining things or they were actually occurring. It was about this time I discovered Yvonne Smith, while reading an article about her in UFO Magazine. She was local and formed an organization called CERO. Close Encounters Research Organization. I wanted to contact her and work with her on my experiences. The big concern was Gilly.

Gilly was a big skeptic on the subject. She didn't discount it; she was fascinated by it, but was holding out until the jury got in, despite being with me numerous times and witnessing UFOs that were clearly not our aircraft. She always thought they were. She knew I had a lot of knowledge about human aircraft but so many times when we would see a UFO she would tell me that I didn't know for sure, even when it was a disc, with no NAV lights or makings, wings or visible signs of propulsion, even when it burst into a bright object lighting up the sky and sped off at unbelievable rate of speed. I called it denial. How could I go to someone like Yvonne and spend time with them, have hypnosis sessions and investigative work done, without alarming her and come under criticism from my own wife. This worried me a great deal.

Chapter Twenty:
My Art

I started illustrations and masks of the various visitors described in the books I was reading during the mid- seventies. One of these books was Travis Walton's famous account of his encounter "Fire in the Sky". I remember looking at the drawings in his famous book and feeling a familiarity with them. It was 1975 and I just had to sculpt what I saw in his book and make a mask. Not so much to wear but to have a full-sized sculpture. I made a clay sculpture, as I would for any film project, mask sized and molded in plaster. I made the actual mask out of Latex and painted it exactly as it was in his book.

The sculpture haunted me really. This was 12 years before Communion and, despite everything I had experienced, I still wasn't connecting the dots yet. I wanted to do a different version of the being. Something I felt it may look like more and that lead to my making this mask that used a couple of years later in a Charlie Band movie called, "End of the World". Ironically I ended up playing the alien. Later on I would play Aliens again.

These early versions of what is now known as the grey types had irises and pupils. The black eyes were not commonly described yet. In fact, in my experience, when the Visitors have been close up, I could just see thought the black eyes to the eyes behind, what I think are covers. I think they were something protecting their eyes and or giving them overlaid imagery of data. But it's only a theory. I could see movement behind the dark coverings.

One of my earliest drawings I could find was done in the seventies, although I didn't understand why I changed the date all these years later. I changed the date to 1980.

You can see at the top, in the same pencil I drew the picture that it was 1970. What I recall now is that I did make this drawing in 1970 but later found it and dated it when I found it in red pen since the old date was fading. Clearly the eye's have the slanted look we know today.

Over the years leading up to the nineties I did a lot of masks and versions of these beings for TV shows and film. I even started a company called *Dreamland Effects,* where I produced sculptures of the grays and artwork I sold to the public through UFO Magazine.

Notice the now black eyes and the more pointed chin. This is the image that became iconic and the media and public ran with.

If you ever wondered where it began it was right here. This was the very same bust that Chris Carter put on his desk in front of me when he interviewed me to work on X-Files. I tried to introduce myself and he said, "Sit down Steve. I know who you are", while putting two of my busts on his desk. But it wasn't until I started going to Yvonne that I started obsessively doing more and more art and sculpture. As I recalled my experience I could see them better. Hypnosis was helpful in getting a better look at the

Visitors than I have had at this point. Yvonne asked me to illustrate my experiences and also of those in her group. I must have done hundreds of drawings and paintings over the next few years.

This was a painting I did for Yvonne's lectures. Notice the now frail bodies and super pointed chin. The taller leader type has huge eyes that have that mantis look. It's presenting a small fetus to the woman on the table. This was an experience one of Yvonne's clients had. But the look was based on my own experience.

This image was based on a feeling I had, an image in my head that when I was in the crib I had someone always watching me. When I showed this to the CERO group they all reacted to it, as it seemed to remind of something they experienced themselves.

These images were used on talk shows Yvonne appeared on, and later, shows I would appear on. The TV show "Sightings" approached me to use my art and sculptures and later contracted me to build puppets of the grays that could be animated and used in different episodes.

This was done for "Sightings" and the puppet was fully animated.

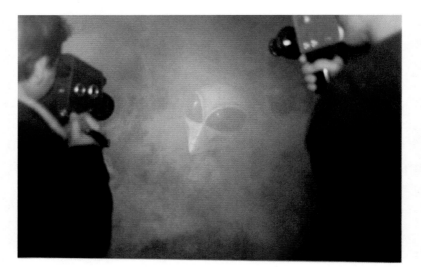

Another shot taken on that night where the being was being filmed with cameras as thought they had just found it.

They also had me make some wearable masks that I later sold through my company. They sold very well especially since they were used on "Sightings "which was a very popular show.

Today I find my masks being auctioned on E-Bay. Here's one I just found in a search on E-bay.

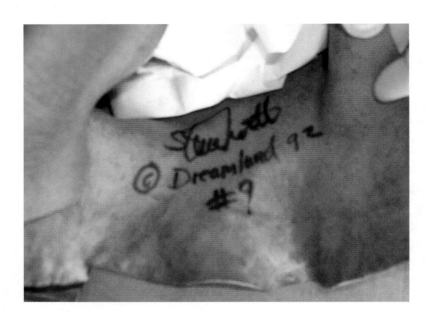

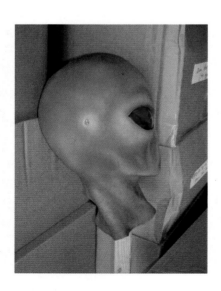

In fact "High Times" contacted me a bought a mask to use on their cover of the magazine

Later I did a show for Whitley called "NBC's Con-firmation". It was a two-hour special on the subject of UFO's and abduction. The production contracted to make the Visitor puppets for their reenactments.

At this point in my career, I have done more work on this subject than anyone else has ever done. I lost track of a lot of it and have very little to show for it today, outside of a few paintings and mostly slides I took of everything I have ever done. Fortunately I was able to find a lot of it on the Net. It's still being used today. In fact some people have even used some of the busts and took pictures of them to pass them off as real images.

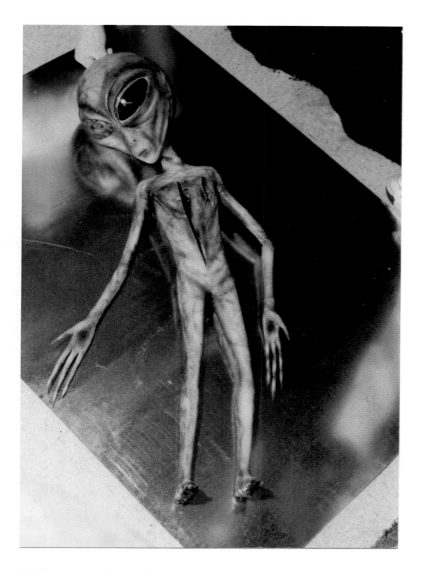

This was done for a show that showed a gray autopsy. I had done several full sized sculptures and puppets.

I also did a line of Communion images because Whitley and Anne were kind enough to give the rights to reproduce the image of the Communion lady. We did T-shirts, a mask and I still make today a bust of the Communion Visitor.

Here I am with Whitley at a conference on UFO's in Northern California. You can see in the background a full sized Communion bust, the T-shirt and some of my artwork at my booth.

This was the painting I did for the T-shirt.

The bust we still have on our website today. And lastly the full sized wearable mask.

Here I am at the first Granada Hills house in my studio. This is actually the clay sculpture before made the mold

I could go on and on with the work I have done and it would make a whole other book. The work was cathartic and fun to do. It helped me face my fears and help others. It was my contribution to this phenomenon, this field of interest and a study I would not return to for many years. When I did, it would be in an all-encompassing form of media and self-expression. To make a TV series about my own experiences that would include everything I have learned in art and my work in Hollywood. "But Something is There" was about to be born.

Chapter Twenty-One
Yvonne Smith

Through Don Ecker, who I told about my experience, I contacted Yvonne. I told Gilly I would be getting involved in her group as an illustrator. I would be her forensic artist and create sketches of the visitors her clients would describe. It wasn't totally true but it also afforded me the opportunity to meet other people who had the experience and, most importantly, tell Yvonne about my own experience, this lead to my having a first meeting with Yvonne to start the procedure of hypnotic regression. Now, I remember clearly telling Gilly about this and the fact I would be doing artwork for Yvonne but Gilly only heard the part she wanted to hear. It would not be until later on that she would grasp that I was in fact having these experiences too.

I thought it was too easy at the time, telling her. I didn't talk at length about it and I assume that by now in our long relationship she would understand I was involved. So time went on. Things continued as usual and weekly I would go see Yvonne. Although I could remember quite a lot, there were parts of events that I didn't. And the hypnosis helped bring these lost memories back. We will go into some of this detail later on, however, the most important point I have to share here is how this can affect even ruin relationships and marriage.

One day Gilly and I were in the kitchen talking. She asked me about the work I was doing with Yvonne. I told her I was doing lots of artwork and enjoyed it. Gilly knew this because I was constantly at it in our home studio. In fact, we started a small company. As said before, I created sculptures of the beings both as busts and full figures. In addition, I made masks and paintings. We were selling these through UFO Magazine. She enjoyed our company that we named, "Dreamland Effects" and we were making money with the art. One day we were talking about my work with Yvonne. I told her the hypnosis work I was doing with her helped contribute to the look of the beings and success of our little company. She stopped me cold. She couldn't understand why I was doing hypnosis. I told her again. "I am having these experiences and have had them since I was a child".

She absolutely lost it. Claimed I had never told her this. She was so upset she made me feel ill. She was just hysterical. This is what I was hoping to avoid and it reminded me of "Close Encounters" and the Carrie Garr character, only worse. I remember clearly her exact words. She said to me, "if I was having these experiences I must be scared out of my mind Oh my God!" The truth is I wasn't at all. Not out of my mind, and I think that was the key word. She feared her husband's mental health was in question and it frightened her.

Gilly and I would talk at length about life after to death, ghosts, UFO and other paranormal subjects in the past. She had many different opinions about it all. But on one subject she had a clear position. When you die and your brain stops functioning, you are no longer. That was the tip of the iceberg. She didn't feel these things could actually be happening to her husband, or that there could be an undefined intelligence contacting humans. It was just too far-fetched. She was very suspicious of Yvonne and the entire community with which I was involved. My work with the art and sculptures started gaining widespread popularity and it was benefiting us. People having these experiences saw in my art what they had experienced as being the same. We started getting a lot of snail mail from people telling us this and thanking us for the art.

It led to almost every TV show in town on the subject contacting me for my masks of the beings, full-sized puppets to use in their recreations and my artwork. If you remember the grays on "Sightings", then you saw my work. As they found out about my work with Yvonne and my personal experiences, they asked me to go on camera to talk about it. I was reluctant to do so because of Gilly. I knew it would make her uncomfortable and it did. But it also led to more and more opportunity for our Dreamland FXs business too. So she put up with it. And I did more and more shows as a result.

I was even contacted by X Files for the pilot epi-sode to make the aliens for their show. Paul Rab-win, the producer of X Files, called me. Paul asked me to come to the Fox back lot for an interview about a new TV series about UFOs and Aliens that no one had heard about it before not even me. When I arrived I met the team. Then I was asked to go to Chris Carter's office, as he wanted to talk further. I came into his office and he told me to take a seat. I started to introduce myself and as I did, he stopped me and told me he knew me. As he did this, he reached down below his desk and pulled out two of my grey visitor busts and sat them on his desk giving me a big grin. We had a great talk. Chris knew a lot of about the subject. He gave me the script for the pilot and asked me to read it and get back to him. I did get back to him, but unfortunately, they were moving the production to Canada and they could not bring me along. Canadian laws do not allow Americans to work on productions when they have Canadians that do the same work. I don't know if it is true today, but it was at that time. Still my art and some sculptures appeared in the show as set dressing throughout the shows history.

I was also asked to give lectures with my art on my experiences to UFO conventions. Yvonne made it possible to get wide spread attention about my experiences and artwork. I kept going to Yvonne for a long while and we had many sessions. I learned a lot and connected with the community. All this helped me come to terms with my experience and learn to live with it. I would continue to have sessions with Yvonne for a few years still to come. I have a hard time remembering just how many. We reviewed many of my lost memories that were similar to those of others'. What I learned in her support group meetings is that the experience, and how it's perceived by each individual, is shaped by how one is raised, one's religion or faith they were taught and one's level of education. But there were always benchmarks that were the same. How the visitors appeared, what the craft looked like, and many of the procedures and interactions were identical. But how they perceived the experience was different. Some viewed this experience as a threat, abduction against their will, a nightmare or even demons. But many others viewed this as a grace, something that uplifted them into a world of wonder. It is life's journey in search of our very souls.

Out of many sessions with Yvonne and looking back at them I was frightened, worried and even apprehensive about my experience. It is clear in some of the transcripts and tapes of my regressions. Always I viewed this as something I wouldn't trade away for a life of bliss. This was my connection to that greater reality so many live without. I think looking back now that most of the unpleasantness of all this was due to the reaction of my friends and family. It wasn't good and caused me a lot of unnecessary stress and apprehension. Human beings frighten me more than any other single aspect of my experience. I was searching my name on the net and stumbled across this transcript from one of my sessions with Yvonne. It is a good example of the many I had with her. I do remember this well, to this date, and in reading, I still remember very well.

In researching a witnesses accounting from memory of an event, we look to the same event being retold. We look to see if it changes at all. Gets bigger and grows into more. But in most cases we find that even years later these people will recount with no degradation at all the exactly the same the memory of the said event.

This has been true in my case and this is one of those cases. Before I read it again, after so long I could still recall what occurred exactly.

This is an exact transcript of the recording:

Yvonne Smith, Certified Hypnotherapist

Transcript #551

Subject: Steve Neill

YS: OK, Steve, we're going to be leaving these mountains for just a little while, knowing that you can always go back there. It's always there. It's very, very special. And now we're going to be taking a very short trip back in time. To explore a memory or a possible experience that you may have had. As we leave now, the present time, of January 19th, 1994, you allow yourself now to begin to drift back in time, very gently, very slowly, to Saturday night, December 18th, 1993. Gently drift back to that night. That night, December 18th, 1993. As you left the wedding and you went back home. And as you describe now what you did on that night. As you speak verbally, the deeper asleep you will become.

SN: Well, I'm just getting in the house. And, uh, (name) lets me in.

YS: What time is it, Steve?

SN: I don't see a clock. I don't think I'm really paying attention to the time. It's about a little after 12, I think. The, uh, channel 36 is still on. I guess they fell asleep listening to the radio program. (Name) goes to bed, and (name) sort of wakes up, and I, uh, try to tell her about the wedding. Talked about the ceremony. But she's not really paying attention. She's really out. I could hardly keep her awake. I don't exactly remember what I do after that. I know that I get the bed ready, the bedroom ready, and I put her to bed. I know (name)'s gonna be calling me on the way home, so I want to get her to bed and get the phone in the other room, my shop, so the phone doesn't wake her up when it rings. And I put her to bed, and put a movie on for her, on the video. And we talk a little bit more about the evening, but she drifts off. The sound is real loud in the house. The old favorite sound. I go to the shop, which is what I always do. Close the door, and uh, (name) calls. I think it's after 1 o'clock. I'm sitting in my big tall chair talking to (name) on the phone. And we talk all the way 'til she gets home. I remember her telling me that they were walking in the house, attending to her dogs and stuff. And we had a really good conversation. Really good time ... After that, I just kind of sit in the shop for a while. And I look at some of my things I've been working on. Thinking about what I'm gonna do next, but the minute I start thinking that, I keep thinking of more reasons to stay awake. I feel really good but just, like everything's just OK, and (unheard) having a good time And I close up the shop It' s after 2 now. Lock the hop door end turn off the fireplace. Check the back door make sure it's locked. Check all the animals and male sure they are in. And I come into the bedroom. The TV is still on. (Name)'s sound asleep. I turn everything off and go to bed myself. I'm just laying there and looking around the room, like I always do. Kind of wondering. I always wonder. Pull the covers up close over, over my chin. Very tired, and dismally trying to tell myself that if anything happens I will remember it. I will remember it - Mmm ... Thought I heard something.

YS. What did you hear?

SN: Like the house shook, or something. Like a sonic boom, or something ... I'm seeing light. Seeing light through my eyelids. My eyes are closed but I'm seeing, I'm seeing light through them. Like it's moving around. I hear somebody talking about me.

YS: What are they saying?

SN: Someone's talking to someone else. I feel the covers coming off. My eyes are still closed. I don't know why I don't open (unheard). Pull the covers off and I feel cold. It's like two people talking to each other. But I can't, I can't make out what they're saying. Something about moving me. There's some, there's some difference of opinion of something. About where they should bring me. Somebody's got

124

a very cold touch. My eyes are opened just a crack. There's someone right there. Right there, looking at me.

YS: How close?

SN: Inches away. He's, he's tryin' to figure out if I'm awake or not. I hear him say, or think, "He's awake, barely." I'm not, they're pulling me. I feel like a. like I'm weighing so much. So heavy. Like I'm limp. My head kind of snaps back. So weird. Hand on my back. Hand on my arm. They want me to move. He's saying to me, "Come on, move. Come on.

YS: Can you see what they look like?

SN: Yes.

YS. What do they look like?

SN: The usual. The small one's. Although they seem really big because the head's so close to me. I think they look the same. They don't look menacing or threatening in any way. Almost like cute little creatures. Inquisitive and very full of self-importance. It's very important to them that they do this right. Whatever it is. I know that my hand is asleep, my arm's asleep. It's numb. Can't feel my fingers. I don't know why. They got me sitting up in bed and they're trying to get me out of bed. This is different somehow, because, ya know, other times they just lift me out so easily. It's very hard to understand. I'm confused for a second as to whether I was waking up to go to the bathroom. And I was standing there, trying to get my balance. But I know that it's not what it is because these guys are here. We walk down the hallway. We're walking down the hallway. There's two of them. I can see the kitchen. And there's bright light coming through the kitchen sliding door. There's curtains, the curtains are hanging. There's air blowing the curtains back. The sliding door is open. The plant room's really lit up. It's cold. The air coming in is cold. We, we walk. I think we walk to the curtain. I think it gets pushed aside. Or maybe it rubs against me. And it gets pushed aside. I can see the color of it because the light is backlighting it. and it's kind of purply. But it's the color of the fabric. We go into the plant room. The light's really bright in the back yard. We're outside. We' re outside. I don't think we opened the door. Things are real, not very in focus. It's hard to see. I feel like I'm sedated. We're standing outside on the concrete, the walkway, by the tree. And I look up to see where the light's coming from. But I know where it's coming from. It just all seems so familiar. Started to feel really shaky. And I don't like this feeling. Wish I could be calmer. But I think part of it's just that it's cold, and I'm just in my underpants, and my T-shirt. It's cold. Oh. I don't feel so heavy anymore. Oh, this part feels kind of good. I'm just cold, though. Oh, I feel cold. Oh, that light's bright when I look up at it. Just a bright light in the sky. It's solid. Doesn't move. Right past the tree. Right past the tree. I could touch it. Oh ... Oh... Oh ...

YS: Are you still standing there?

SN: No, we've, we've gone up. We're up high. We go right into this light. I think we enter a doorway. I don't feel so cold. We're inside. We're not inside where I thought we'd be. This is different. This is really different

YS: Can you describe it?

SN: Yeah- Looks like a hospital. I've seen this corridor before. Smooth, polished floor. White walls. Looks like fluorescent lights mounted on the ceiling. Plastic grids or something. This is not where I thought we'd be. Two of the little ones are with me. I have to go to the bathroom so bad. I wish this wouldn't happen.

YS: Just take a deep breath

SN: They're moving me to a doorway on the left. Oh, God. Darn. Oh.

YS: (Unheard)

SN: Yes. I'm in some sort of doctor's office, room. It looks like an operating room.

YS: Can you describe what you see In there?

SN: Looks like an operating room. Looks like a human operating room. It's a metal table, instruments. I don't believe I'm seeing this. This is like their place. There's a light, examination light. I've seen these kind. Oh, I can't get past my bladder. It's hurting so bad. Damn it.

YS: Try to focus on the experience. The (un-heard) bladder is trying to distract you.

SN: I know. It just hurts so bad.

YS: Try to focus on what you re seeing.

SN: They're tryin' to put me on the table. They put me on the table, butt first, and they push me down. I'm trying to resist. I'm scared 'cause I don't like this room. It's not like other rooms I've been in. I hear voices speaking. That's not theirs. They're try-ing to push me down. One of them got my T-shirt. And he starts pulling it up, and it, and it, he pull It up so hard my arms automatically go up, like they're limp. It pulls off. Oh. The other one Pulls my under-pants off. This reminds me of being at the doctor's for surgery. They're pulling my arm out. And they're putting like straps on my wrists. Oh

YS: You can feel the straps on your wrists?

SN Yes. Something around my feet. Like one big one? Oh. oh my bladder hurts so bad.

YS: And how many are there with you?

SN: They're leaving me. The little ones, I think they're leaving me. One checks me to make sure I'm secure. Oh, I've got to go to the bathroom.

YS: You've got to go now?

SN: Oh yeah. It is just so painful.

YS: You re going to be able to get up

SN: I haven't felt it like this in a long time.

YS: You're going to be able to get up, open your eyes, and without awakening from your hypnotic state, and carefully go to the bathroom. And come back and resume your experience. (Subject goes to bathroom) Ok, (name), take a deep breath, now. Knowing now that you're safe. And you're exploring. You felt yourself now on the table, and they're leaving you.

SN: This table, it's stainless steel. Kind of raised lip around it. I can see that when they're bringing me in. I've seen this kind of table before. They' re putting me on the table. I can hear people talking about me. Mmm. I guess it's a little cold in here. Mmm. I know there's people in the room. I don't see them. The room's not dim or anything, It's kind of evenly lit. I heard somebody, something dropped or crashed. I have a really hard time believing what I'm seeing.

YS: Just describe everything you're seeing, experiencing.

SN: It's, it's just, it's - It's, oh. There's a man standing to my right, talking, talking.

YS: What does the man look like?

SN: He's talking to one of them. I think I've seen him before. He's. uh, well, he's wearing a white smock. He's got an ID badge on his pocket.

YS Can you read what the ID badge says?

SN: No, it's to my. . . He' s tending to my side. I can just see it. I think there's a picture on it. He sees me look at him. He's, he's dark haired, but he's balding. Mustache. Dark mustache. I don't like him. I just don't like that he's here. I don't like that they're here. I don't like this. (Unheard). This is not right. He's talking to this being. I don't, I don't hear the beings, in back. I can see how much shorter the being is in contrast to him. Ow! Something jabbed me in my arm.

YS: What part of your arm?

SN: My upper shoulder. My left shoulder.

YS: Your left shoulder?

SN: Mm-hmm.

YS: Can you see what it was that was used?

SN: No, when I looked to see what happened, someone was just walking away. Oh, oh! Oh, that feeling.

YS: How do you feel?

SN: Almost kind of good.

YS: (Unheard)

SN: But I hear voices. Things are kind of spinning. I can't focus. I feel ... I see like images, people images. None of this makes any sense. Of them looking at me, in darkness. Like through water or something. And the chatter. Chatter of voices. Although I can't distinguish anything. It's just muddle. I'm aware of people. I'm aware of people pushing at me. Touching me. My eyes are open a bit now. I feel like I've been asleep for awhile or something. I still feel real drugged. Then someone's shining like a little penlight in my eye, or something. And there's someone standing real close, in my face again, saying something about, "He's awake. He's awake." I'm aware of two other people standing over me. They're tall, and they're wearing like blue outfits, They're doctors. They have masks across their face, and they've got caps on.

YS: They look human?

SN: They're human. At least they look. human. The little one says something to them. I think they have an air sound. The sound I described before. It's like a hiss. I'm just aware that there's something in my nose.

YS: What is -

SN: He put something in my nose. I don't know. It's like a tube. I think that's the noise. Like oxygen going in my nose. I feel like I'm waking up. One of the doctors has glasses on. They're not wire-rimmed. They're black. He's got something in his hand.

YS: Can you see what's in his hand?

SN: It's like a little metal ball, in the being's hand. The doctor has some long thin instrument. Like a butter knife, or something. Looks like metallic. One grabbed my head. Because I'm moving around too much for him. He's saying, "Hold his head. Hold his head." Pushing the metal (unheard) to the right. And strapping my head down. Putting something around my head. Oh God, this is -

YS: What's he putting around your head?

SN: Feels like a leather strap or something. Something that they can tighten down. Makes it very hard for me to move. The doctor touches this metal thing to my head. It feels really cold. It feels really cold. Oh. I can't see anything, He's blocking all the light.

YS: Do you feel pain?

SN: It hurts. But it's like - . It's like if someone took a piece of dry ice and stuck it on your head, and just left it there, left it there. It's so numb, it hurts. It makes my skull ache. It's like it's burning, but I know it's not burning. I don't like this.

YS: Do you still have that feeling in your head?

SN: Yes. I can't move. He's saying something to somebody. I can't make it out. He just keeps holding it there. Oh, it hurts. I keep wondering when he's going to take it away. He's going to take it away any minute, I know it. It just keeps sitting there.

'(S Is he the only one touching you;

SN I don't know. I think someone has my arm. I don't know why. I can't move my wrist. I feel like it's trying to comfort me. All I can think of at the time is, "How can you let them do this to me? How can you let them touch me?" Ow! God. He hasn't moved that thing. I can't feel anything in my forehead. Although it felt like, like a little part of my skin came with it. It's numb and feels cold and it hurts. I tried to catch what that was. They said something and I just can't make it out. I want to know what they're doing.

YS: Can you move your head?

SN: No. They're loosening the strap, and they're moving my head from the right side, to straight up, and straight up. The doctor's looking at it, touching it and saying, "That's good. Now, that's good." And he says something to this, I guess it's the taller one, on my left. It's got these metal, it's got something in its hand. It's hard to describe it. It's palm-sized, little smaller. It's round, highly polished chrome ball. In a circle. It's attached to some kind of plate, (unheard) plate. I can't see the rest of it 'cause he's palming it. In the center it's, it's dark. But there's a protrusion. There's - . For some reason, I get the feeling that the protrusion, it's narrow and it's turned, like it turns. I can see a little movement in it. I know he's gonna put it on my head. It's like, this is the part of this that he's supposed to do. I can feel the pressure of it sitting on my head. He's very careful about the way he places it.

YS: Where does he place it on your head?

SN: On the same spot. Same spot. It still feels pretty cold. I mean, it feels cold. My bone feels frozen. My skull. I hear a sound. A whirling sound. Oh!

YS: What's happening?

SN: Oh! Oh!

YS: Describe what's happening, Steve...

SN: Something's going in!

YS: In that spot?

SN: Yeah ! Oh

YS: Take some deep breaths, Steve. Just exploring, you're doing fine,

SN: Oh, it feels so. . . (Moans) Somebody's got my arm. One's putting his hand on. Might be the one standing over me on my head. Saying it won't hurt me. but it hurts! Owe! Maybe it's the idea. Damn, it hurts. They've got something in my skull. In my brain, I think. Damn! Damn, it hurts! Hurts.

I've gotta stop thinking, I've gotta put my mind somewhere. Damn it hurts.

YS: Is he still holding it on?

SN: Yes! He's saying it's not supposed to hurt. He's got his hand on me. I think it's - - He's telling me I gotta let go. I gotta relax.

YS: (Unheard)

SN: It'll be over in a minute.

YS: (Unheard) pain and discomfort. Just record everything that happens.

SN: It's stuck in my head. I get the feeling that they're putting something in. Oh! Oh! It's there for so long! I tried to - . He's telling the doctor something. The doctor's saying something to him. "We've got to get that out pretty soon. Ow! Oh, it still hurts. It retracted. I felt something retract. It's funny, I didn't notice this before, but the balls, before when they touched my head, were cold, now they're warm. Oh God, this thing hurts. He's takin' it off. He's saying, "See, that wasn't so bad." I don't' know why he's saying that. It was horrible. It was like having someone put a cork screw in your head. A very fine one. I try to look at the thing as it's pulled away. I don't see anything. It's like, it just looks the same. I don't see any blood. He moves it away very fast.

YS: It's got blood on it?

SN: No, I don't see any blood. Oh, my neck. My neck's so stiff. Oh! Oh! Oh, they release the strap on my head. One of the doctors is dabbing my head, with a cotton something. Antiseptic. I smell it. Oh.

YS: Can you smell the antiseptic'?

SN: Oh, I can smell it. He's rubbing the spot. He's concerned that it marked pretty bad. He's a little irritated that it marked so bad. I don't think he wants it to show. He keeps dabbing it over and over again. When he pulls it away, I can see a little, I see reddish, pale red, and a lot of yellow. Pink and yellow. It's gross. And he takes another swab and rubs it some more. It's like he's really concerned that it shows too much. He says it right to the little one, the being at my side, he says, "He's gonna know something happened." He's pissed off at them. "I didn't think it would show like this", he says. Oh. He keeps dabbing it. Last time he dabs he pushes hard, and says, "That's as good as it gets." When he was doing this, I noticed that he wasn't wearing like an operating suit. This guy was in a smock and no mask. I'm trying to look at his ID badge. It's got big black lettering to the side of his picture. I can even make out the background of his picture. Red background. Curtains or something. I wanna say looks like an N, A? I can't make out the last of it. N, A?

YS: You can see very sharp and clear.

SN: C, A? Something like that. My eyes. If I could just blink and get the goo out of my eyes. There's some smaller writing underneath. Something either "Expired" or "Restricted" and a number: 212. Something like that. There's a signature on it. I can't read the handwriting. I get the feeling it's his signature.

YS: Is his name printed anywhere? Focus in on it. Is his name printed anywhere on it?

SN: I, I can't see a thing. I see other lettering. I can't make it out. The biggest lettering is the N and the A, that I'm sure of. There's a black line under it. Pin (unheard). Metallic blue, metal pin. Silver clip. This guy's about early 40's.

YS: He has a mask on?

SN: No, no mask. He's been cleaning my head. He's the one that's mad. Or I think is annoyed. I don't know what happened to me. I don't know. I didn't, I guess I didn't pay attention. MY head hurts. It hurts. It stings. I looked over and there's a big being there. And I ask, ya know, "Why did you do this? And it says, something, "It's important." And that it will help me, somehow.

YS: What does that big being look like? Is he tall? Is he (unheard)?

SN: I think so. It must be. It's hard to tell. I'm laying on my back. My head is raised. But as I look over, the head is so much larger than the smaller one. I don't know if it's, I guess it is the same one that I'm used to seeing. It's her, I think. She acts concerned. I think she's concerned.

YS: That you hurt?

SN: That it hurt, yes. That they hurt me so much. But that it really was a good thing that they did. I just keep hearing the same thing over and over again. That sort of patronizing tone. "This'll help you. This'll help you." And, ya know, I was very good, and all those things. I feel like I'm being patronized. I feel like I'm being humored. Oh, God that thing stings. It stings so much. They're loosening the straps on my feet. It feels good. I had my ankles so close together. And my wrists. I don't know why I just don't get off this table and run. But it's like, somehow I just know that I'm supposed to lay here. I know what to do. I don't know where I'd run. I don't know where I'd go. I (unheard) what they're doing. I mean, that's what I have to assume. It just seems so nonchalant to them. They're going about their business. The big one's walked around to my right side. It's talking to the same doctor. Wish I could make out the rest of that badge.

YS: Is he the only human you see?

SN: At the time, yes, yeah. I don't, no, I don't see Two small ones, one of them's leaving the room. Also, I noticed something else. The light's are dimmer in the room now. They're not as bright at all. And I'm kind of glad for that because they were really hurting my eyes. In fact, I remember now they, they had that light, examination light over my head. 'Cause I remember it being really bright, And it's dimmer now, in the room. They're saying, "Can you get him up now?" The doctor's saying, "Do you think it's a good idea to get him up now?" Because I'm so groggy and so drugged still. And I think to myself, "If they re worried about that, why don't they just- float me?" They've done that before. But they don' t. They just kind of, they're very strong. They come around and help me up. My legs drag off the table and just kind of dangle. I get a lot of encouragement about, "You can do it. Come on, you've gotta get up." The doctor says he's gotta go wait for some-one, for some appointment, or something. It's so weird because he's talking to these beings like he's almost in charge of them. He says something about, "Sure. Everything's OK. You guys are OK without me now. I've gotta go to this other appointment." Or something likes that. And kind of starts to walk and he turns back and he looks at me. He just kind of looks at me. He doesn't smile or anything, he just looks at me. I said something to him, but I can't put my finger on it. He leaves. The hallway's brighter lit. I can see 'cause the door's open. The little one just hands me my T-shirt. "Just put it on." I mean, I can hardly move my arms. They help me put my under-pants back on. I sort of bend over and they put the T-shirt out of my hand and over my head. I put my arms through it. It feels good because it's cold Feels good to have any clothes on. I just don't like being cold like that. They just start to walk but somehow I feel that I'm not really walking this time. I'm trying to, but my feet are dragging. I can feel the floor on the backside of my toes. And (unheard). Oh, like scratching on a blackboard. Oh. Oh. I actually said something to them. "Pick my feet up!" God, that's awful. I can see the floor. It's like some kind of stone. It's got some kind of texture to it. It's not like you can feel, but you can see. We went to the end of this hallway into this - . Oh, I've seen this before. This is a big cavern. Big open expanse, supported by beams. Big metal girders. And it's very high, the ceiling. There's a corridor to my left and there's a yellow white light coming from it. There's some light over the top of it, with one of those metal screens around it. And I want to say the lights are red or orange or something. There's a sign, too. It's too far away to read. It's very dark in there. They're taking me right for this corridor. It's weird! We've been going to this corridor, and it's really bright, yellow light. Really bright. Bright, white yellow. Just bright. It's so bright I can't see anything else. I wonder what's going to happen. We just keep going' and going'. I could just see the top of my house for a second. It was like it came out of this wh. . . It's very difficult to describe. Came out of the white light, yellow white light. 'Cause it's definite yellow to it. It was like a hole left in it and through the hole was like a projection and it was 3-dimensional. I entered right into it and now we're above my house, descending to it. Definitely the backyard. I see the bars on my bedroom window. And it's light. It's lit up. There's light on them. Descending. Screen door's open. And the plant room. And just like Peter Pan, just float right down to it. Right to the (unheard). Right into the plant room. Back to the sliding door. The kitchen. Down the hallway. I see my bed and I see it really well because that blue light coming through the curtains. My wife's lying there in bed she's out. Her eyes are slightly open. Looks terrible. Her eyes are open like, but she's not awake. They put me in bed. I just get in and pull the covers up. Two of them leave. Always, one looks back at me before it disappears down the hallway. I'm getting kind of used to them, they don't really scare me. They disappear down the hallway. (Sigh)

YS: (Unheard)

SN: I'm awake now. I can see the clock, too. 4 o'clock. (Unheard) when I first woke up I expected it to be light in the room, but it's not. I feel relieved. My head hurts. I feel weird, like I was under sedation. I just, I wanna get up. I wanna get up and go in the kitchen. Drink some water. And I get those overwhelming impressions that I don't need to get up. I need to sleep. I don't need to think about anything. I just need to forget about all this and go back to bed. Just go to sleep. But there's nobody there. I just feel this, what I hear. Or what I sense. Don't hear it, I sense it. I try to pull my leg out of the bed and it just won't move. I get it as far as the edge of the bed. I just realize it's useless.

YS: OK, (name), we're going to leave this (unheard) now. Just take a deep breath now. As we leave that time and coming back very, very gently and slowly to the present' time of January 13, 1994. Just slowly and gently go back to those beautiful mountains. Feeling very, very peaceful and calm. Just feel yourself going back to those mountains, knowing that as you re there in the mountains you begin to feel very much at ease. And let me know when you're there.

SN: I think I'm back.

YS: Doing just fine. Taking deep breaths now. Take those deep breaths. Feel your entire body very comfortable. Very good, very calm.

SN (Unheard)

YS: Knowing now that no matter what you've experienced in the past or what you might experience in the future, you're able now to put it all into perspective in your life. Incorporate all this into your life, knowing that there's a whole group of people around you who care about you, who listen to you, who help you. And you in turn help all the new people coming. And knowing now that your talent and your art work have a definite purpose in this life. And tonight when you sleep, and each and every night you will find you begin to experience a restful uninterrupted sleep, knowing that sleep is very important to you and your work. You rest your body and your mind. As you wake up each and every morning feeling rested, energetic, and ready to meet the challenges of each new day. Look forward to your work and all the good things that come to you. As I count from zero back up to five, you will awaken feeling fully refreshed, mentally alert, very calm, with a good sense of well being and feeling great. Starting with zero, (claps), which always represents deep sleep, and the suggestions I have given you are now reinforced, as you're coming up to one, and two, as your breathing becomes more normal, three, just feel your body starting to come around, four, your eyes open, and five, wide awake. Feeling great. One, two, three, four, five, eyes open, wide awake. Feeling great. Very calm. Very restful. Feeling great. One, two, three, four, five. Wide awake. I think maybe, how about, let's get that part of your head x-rayed.

SN: It stings. It hurts.

YS: Well, you went through the memory. Did it feel very real to you? What's that -

SN: Yeah, especially that part where they had that thing on my head. It was like ice cold.

YS: Do you think you can draw, um, draw a picture of the, of that instrument, and -

SN: Yeah, it was real plain.

YS: And you know, the other one that they used?

SN: Yeah.

YS: I mean in the beginning-

SN: The top of Billy Meier Jell-O mold space saucer or. . .

YS: Oh, that one? With the round balls on it?

SN: Round balls, but it wasn't a saucer. But - metal plate balls on it around it, like that. Looked like that. Had this thing in the middle.

YS: Just draw it.

SN: Made a noise.

YS: You should have a drawing of the instruments anyway. What about that, the human doctor, though? That's bizarre.

SN: Yeah. It's not the first time I've seen them. Although we've never had a session on it. This was the first one we've done where the. But I mean, in my dreams, I told you that the tent, the examination booths, whatever it was. Saw doctors in there. Oh boy, I feel wobbly,

YS: Yeah, that thing about the humans, um -

SN: Oh, I don't like that.

YS: Makes me very concerned.

SN: I don't like that.

YS: You know it's -

SN: The way he was talking to them, like -

YS: Well, it's like one thing of being, ya know, poked and prodded by someone who's not of this earth, ya know -

SN: He was colder than they were.

YS: But the thought of human's involved. I know I've heard a lot of reports about that.

SN: Me, too. But I've just never really wanted to believe it.

YS: I don't have that many in my caseload. So it's like, ya know, ya hear it and you kind of file it, and -

SN: He was a cold bastard. You know, I felt - I couldn't feel anything from him. I feel something from them.

YS: You feel more. like from that female?

SN: You feel, you hear what they think. You feel, you feel what they're feeling, and they, or they, and they try, they comfort you and stuff.

YS: He was like just -

SN: "Hold his head! Hold his head!" Ya know, and I don't know if it was him that was strapping me. I don't think it was because it felt gentle, and it got tight, though. It went on and then I felt kind of "mmm", and then my neck was feelin' really bad. But I got the feeling that my head was over this way, so that he could - - 'Cause he was on this side so he could touch this thing there. And then that was done and they could put my head back over this way. Yeah. And that shot, too.

YS: It was in your shoulder?

SN: Sting! yeah, yeah.

YS: But did anything stay there? It was just like they, they put a shot...

SN: I've had that before.

YS: ...there, and that was it?

SN: Yeah. And then I felt real (mumbles), ya know?

YS: I might have other, in other sessions, other people have reported like a shot or something in that part, high up in the shoulder.

SN: Yeah? Yeah, I've seen marks from this when I felt like had something like that, I've had little blood, and little -

YS: What part of the shoulder was it?

SN: Right, right here.

YS: See, and other people said like right in through here.

SN: My arm was like this, and all of a sudden, prick! And "Owe!", and someone was walking away like that.

This was in 1993. And this was one hell of a busy year for the whole phenomenon. And I could share many of these with you but they are so typical. And many of the events that would happen were related more to the physical than the spiritual. Spiritual events are far more significant in my experience than the physical, which I'll share with you later on in this book.

Chapter Twenty-Two
The Coronado Mass Encounter

Another event was so large with the CERO group that Yvonne wrote a book about it. I highly recommend you read her book because it is an excellent accounting of that weekend. It is titled, "Coronado". We were all invited to a Conference in San Diego that was held at the Coronado Hotel in March of 1994.

I was very excited about going to this event because many of my friends would be there and I could share my experiences with liked-minded people. I arrived in the evening and went into the Hotel and had dinner with Yvonne and some of the CERO group. We had a great time and later took a self-tour of the old grand hotel. Many of us shared a room with another CERO member. I shared a room with a friend I knew from the group. In the book my name was changed to *Sam* because at the time Gilly was still here and didn't want me to be part of the book at all. Yvonne changed my name. That night we went to our rooms to sleep. We did not stay in the Coronado but at a smaller hotel nearby. Everything was fine as I got into bed. My friend and I talked for a while and eventually turned off the lights. My friend slept across from me and I could just barely make him out from my vantage point. As I lay there drifting off I noticed a sensation I knew all too well. There was a red light on the ceiling and all of a sudden a strange membrane like material, separated us with a barrier between us. It seemed gelatinous and transparent. There were lights in the room and soon shadows of small creatures. They were here, in force. Something tugged at me. The next thing I knew, I was pulled through the ceiling and into the sky above the hotel. What I remember next was not included in Yvonne's book. I was flat on my back heading towards the dark circle in the sky. It had it's light on both of us. We were slowly going up. There were other lights on us coming from the side. When I turned my head to look, there were helicopters just hovering watching this event happen. These helicopters were most likely military from the nearby air force base on the island called, "North Island Air Station." We were brought up and into the dark shadow and once again inside a structure with lots of rooms and hallways. We were brought to an examination room. I was placed on a table and sat there while they attended to my friend who they conducted procedures on, to his despair. Then they told me I didn't have to have the procedures. They told me I was different from my friend. I won't go into great detail about this encounter. Yvonne's book is worth the read and the whole transcript is there. What I will tell you is this: It wasn't until I started writing this book that I would find out what my friend remembered about the night. Yvonne kept us isolated She asked us not to share with each other what we remembered.

23 years later I read her book and for the first time I found out. He recounted virtually the same experience. And there was more. I always question

the gelatinous membrane because never, in my experience, have I seen or heard of such a thing. Yet, it was experienced by many that night and I had never shared it with them. Yvonne and I, till this day, have remained friends and I often talk to her. In fact, she would later be in the TV pilot, "But Something is There". She still uses my artwork. I think I'm due to make her some new art. I am so grateful to her for her friendship and the work she has done with me. It has relieved my anxiety and allowed me to incorporate this reality into my day-to-day life.

Chapter Twenty-Three

The Support Group

I remember well the first day I went to my first support group meeting at Yvonne Smith's home. It was a little disconcerting. There I was in her living room with about 12 other people I didn't know. Twelve strangers with whom I would soon share, what I thought, were *my* unique experiences. This didn't turn out to be the case. I instead listened to these people tell their stories. These were stories I knew intimately. There were some variations on a theme that differed from mine. These were predominately shaped by an individual's perception of his or her own experiences. In addition to that, the experiences were also shaped by their religious views, upbringing, education and lifestyle. Some saw the experience as a threat. A nightmare with demons bent on taking them and terrifying them. In most cases I found that people that had this perception were raised in a deeply religious setting. Others viewed it as a blessing. This intelligence was trying to raise their consciousness and awareness. This is what makes Whitley Strieber's title "Communion" so fitting. And then there were the people that held out and understandably so. They weren't convinced, even by their own experience, and were hoping for alternate answers. I heard things you will never hear about on the talk shows and media. Many of the people I met never wanted their experience to leave that living room. They wouldn't even talk to their family about it for fear of suffering ridicule. They had no motive to make up such a story as is often suggested by the skeptics, or as I have called them, debunkers.

One of the more amazing things that happened to me in the support group went like this: One day we had a new member introduced to the group. As she walked in, we immediately recognized each other. As she walked into the room, I knew that I had been with her in an experience. Often we would be put together with the opposite sex for intimacy. I remembered her well and it was a bit of an awkward moment to say the least. It's that point where you had hoped that some of these instances were projections from the Visitors. They were masters at it and could make you see, hear, and experience just about anything. But this is one of those shocking moments of confirmation of one's memory and experience.

I heard stories about entire neighborhoods being taken at once. A man in our group woke up one night and looked out his window. On the street below he saw the cigar shaped vehicles in the street. People were being lead out of their homes at night and into the awaiting vehicles. As he looked beyond their street to the intersection, he could see cars drive by. They were completely unaware of the event that was taking place.

Another man told a story about his platoon on a night exercise in the woods when a large dark craft flew over, shined a light on them all, and took the entire platoon. He cried and sobbed as he told this story. It moved us all emotionally. He talked about his commanding officer coming to the barracks after they had been returned. He knew something about what happened and they were told never to talk about it. Many of the men had soiled themselves and were throwing up. Some of men lay on their bunks sobbing or in a daze.

But no matter what I heard, the consistent reporting was about the appearance of the visitors and their craft. Projection though was deep in the experience.

One man I knew talked about a giant rabbit crossing the road in front of his car. It was a dark road and I know the place as I had driven it many times. He was so shocked by what he saw he pulled over to investigate. When he got out he saw lights in an open field. There was some sort of craft there. He went over to get a closer look and when he got right up to it, he saw a 747 airliner just parked there in the field. It was all lit up. He wondered if it could have made an emergency landing but clearly the field was too small for that. He looked to the tail to see if he could identify its origin. That's when he realized that something was wrong because on the tail were numbers. NCC-1701. Now, if you aren't a Star Trek fan, they won't mean much to you, but those are the registry numbers for the USS Enterprise. This was not a 747. And they most likely pulled the registry numbers from his mind and the rabbit. This is what they do.

I could go on for a long time about all the things I heard and saw in the support group. In one respect, nothing I have experienced from my own encounters to reading "Communion" told me more, " But Something is There".

Clearly we were all experiencing something real. But honestly no one knew or knows with what we are dealing. Plenty of people have their theories and conjectures. They had names for the Visitors, grays, reptiles and more but never did any of us really know. The support group was and is a success on many levels because people, in a private setting with others, with the same experience, could at long last talk about it. They know they weren't alone or mentally unsound. And this helped them incorporate this amazing experience into their lives. They could once again live their life without the anxiety, stress, and fear.

Chapter Twenty-Four

The Sound of the Machine

It's hard to remember exactly when, but as I recall it was 1994. One night about 3:00 a.m., I woke up to this sound in the house. It sounded a bit like a 60 cycle hum. It throbbed and moaned and at times reminded me of a didgeridoo. I got up out of bed and looked though the house for its location. Maybe it was our air conditioning or some sort of equipment in the house. As hard as I tried I never did locate the source. The next day I asked Gilly about it. I described it but she had never heard such a sound in the house. I was in the bathroom during the day. It was quiet and I could still hear it. It was not as loud, but definitely there. I then began to notice I could hear it everywhere I went. No matter where I was, at the top of a mountain, at night, or at a friend's house, if it was quiet enough, I could hear it. I wondered if anyone else could hear it. I had friends come over at night, in the quiet, but no one ever heard but me. Now I was starting to wonder if it was all in my mind. But one night I had a friend over and I could just hear it. So I took him in to the quiet of my workshop and had him listen. I didn't describe it to him just asked him if he could hear anything. He could; and when asked to describe it, he did hear exactly as I heard it. I started my quest to find out if anyone else heard this sound before. One night I was watching a show on the Paranormal and the Taos sound of New Mexico was covered in the episode. Then I read about other accounts of it there. I didn't live in Taos. So I looked around and found it wasn't just in Taos and there were other cities and places in the world that heard it. According to studies, only two percent of the world's population could hear the hum. There were all kinds of theories from scientists. The more recent explanation was the movement of the oceans' waves against the shorelines that produced the low hum that is why most of the places it was heard were in coastal locations. But that didn't explain Taos or my being able to her it clearly at eight thousand feet on a mountaintop or in the middle of a desert. Or better yet, at thirty thousand feet in an airplane. No matter where I went, even in Normandy France, I could hear the sound.

Personally I feel the hum is connected to the visitor experience. I would go further to say this is the sound of the machine that generates this simulation, this reality.

The Aboriginal people talked about the Wandjina, who are the spirits of the dreamtime that shape our reality. Their rock paintings, from thousands of years ago, depict beings with large heads and big black eyes. And their didgeridoos I have always thought emulated the sound. The baritone instrument especially did. They sound just like it. I have researched this but never did turn up anything to support my thoughts.

However, if I could talk to a tribal elder, I think I would find I am on the right track. It's just a gut feeling. Science is now just discovering the possibility that we are living in a simulation, a holographic matrix if you will. I believe these people were well aware of it many thousands of years ago, as our own tribal people were here in the United States, South America, and other places around the world. Sometimes it takes science a long time to discover things known by the early peoples of this Earth.

Today all these years later I continue to hear this sound. It never stops. I find it comforting and it doesn't bother me at all. I call it the sound of the machine. Some mornings and nights it's louder and sometimes quieter. It will change pitch and rhythm. It's as if it has a mind and mood of it's own and reflects the mood of our world, our simulation. But always it is there.

Chapter Twenty-Five

Black Helicopters and Strange Men

As I continued on with my life working in film and TV, things started to get even weirder. The experiences were increasing. Things were happening at break- neck speed. I started keeping a journal and writing down everything that happened to me. I took pictures of my body injuries. I kept up the lectures, magazine articles, TV appearances and more. Our Dreamland Effects Company was doing well and we were getting lots of work. But, I started noticing something that wasn't right. It was subtle at first. I noticed dark or black helicopters circling my house. They were unmarked which I knew wasn't right because the FAA requires N numbers on all aircraft. Over time, it increased to alarming levels. One day my wife came home from the store being followed by a very low-flying Bell Jet Ranger. This one was marked and I took pictures of it as I was starting to do. As she pulled into the driveway, it was so low that it got the neighbors attention and they started coming out of their homes; they stood on their porches staring at the bizarre scene. As she brought in the groceries, it got lower and lower. I took many pictures with my camera. Then it backed away and took off leaving the neighbors staring at us as thought we had done something wrong. I thought it might have been a police helicopter but when I called the police about it, they told me they didn't have a police helicopter in Granada Hills. I gave the pictures to a friend of mine that was a pilot at Van Nuys airport. He flew helicopters there and found the helicopter parked. He went in and asked about it and was told it was a rental and anyone could rent it.

Another time I had a friend come by the house around 10:00 at night. My shop was a 3-car garage that had been converted into a studio. It was a wonderful space where I did most of my work. It had a side entrance and often I would have late night visitors from the studios to check on my progress. On that night my friend John stopped by. I could tell he was a little disturbed and asked him what was wrong. He told me as he pulled up he could see someone in the bushes looking through my window. When John got out of the car and approached the house someone suddenly darted out of the bushes and ran past him got into a dark car and speeding off. He told me he was wearing a white shirt and had some sort of ID badge hanging off his pocket.

Another phenomenon was the flashing, as though someone had just taken your picture. This happened often when just leaving out the front door. It happened at restaurants and events and often, they weren't noticed by others or just ignored as one of those things. Despite that on many occasions I had witnesses to this. My phone was tapped. I had all kinds of phantoms and crossover voices. I even had people interrupt my calls and they would tell me I wasn't supposed to be talking about my experience. Clicks, cut calls, beeping you name it, they occurred. Then my mail stopped coming. I just didn't get any for a long time. Bills yes but nothing else and nothing for Dreamland or correspondence with people in the field. It got so bad that Gilly went to the post office and asked the postmaster there about it. He went and checked in the back and brought out an armful of mail that had been held for no apparent reason. She even asked why had this been done. He claimed he didn't know but Gilly kept pressing the issue. He went into the back for a long time, as he had to call someone to find out. When he came back he said he couldn't help her and it was out of his control. She didn't know what that meant, I'm not sure he didn't either but she came home pretty upset. I had people get my phone number and call me to tell me that they had sent in money to buy my art and the mail was sent back to them as return to sender, no such address.

Then mysterious individuals started approaching me at the conferences. One night, an older, very charismatic gentleman approached while I was standing in the back listening to a speaker address-ing a large audience. He showed me his credentials that had very clearly marked on them, CIA. He was quite friendly. He asked me what I was doing here at the convention. That I shouldn't associate with these people. That I should know better. I had agreed long ago not to talk about this. I found this interesting because I never made such an agree-ment that I could recall. Or had I? I thought about this for a long time and then I remembered Mr. Lee telling me that I should never talk about this to any-one. That I would meet others I might talk to but not the public. Is that what he meant? And how could this alleged CIA man know this not unless he had a vested interest in me since the beginning? He was at least in his late sixties and, at that time in my life, he would have been the right age. But again this is just a question or maybe a guess.

Chapter Twenty-Six

Gilly has a Sighting

It's now about 1996. And life has been interesting with all the encounters and my activity on the early Internet and media. I had just made my first website about my own experiences. Life was even strained at home. Gilly never really felt comfortable with all this but we were okay in our relationship. Although she had seen plenty with me, she could always explain away what she saw as being a plane or natural phenomenon. Basically, the idea of the universe being so big and full of unknowns and mysteries frightened her. I understood this but never felt the same way. Although a dark room might frighten me, what might lay inside that room had my curiosity. My curiosity overrode the fear. One night while Gilly and I lay in bed asleep, I awoke to a bright arc-welder-blue object in the sky I could see through our bedroom window. It had this wobble to its movement I had seen before. I got out of bed fast and ran to the window and, as I approached the window, I heard Gilly clearly say, "It's not what you think you can hear the engine". Clearly this wasn't a plane. No lights other than the very bright blue white. But she was right. I could hear a jet engine and it wasn't coming from the blue white light. It was coming from a jet chasing it. I could see the NAVS on the jet and the strobes blinking. I watched as they moved east to west and out of my view. I got back in bed and starred at the window and then it came back, now moving east. The Jet was right behind it and, to my amazement; her daughter was standing in the window watching it. Suddenly the UFO got brighter and skipped across the sky like a rock being skipped on water. It stopped dead and flashed bright blue white in a burst that lighted up the sky like daylight. It was gone and the darkness of night returned. Only the jet remained and faded off into the night. The jet was mostly an F-16 dispatched from Point Mugu. No one said a thing. They had both saw it and went back to sleep. The next morning we were all sitting at the dining room table for tea. Gilly's mom was there. She often came to visit us from England and this was one of those times. We were all pretty quiet. A bit of chitchat but nothing about what we had seen. Then her mother asked me about all the noise she heard coming from my studio at 3:00 in the morning. It woke her up. She told me she had heard me talking to people in the studio. Gilly looked at me and cut me this look. That look you get when someone doesn't want you to talk about something. I just claimed I didn't know what she was talking about; that we were in bed and changed the subject. Gilly never brought this up again and, if she ever did see anything without me, I doubt she would ever tell me. She had to have known what she witnessed that night was unusual and related to my experience. Her daughter knew this too. Still they both continued to doubt my experience.

Chapter Twenty-Seven

Day-time Visits

Gilly had a love for the Renaissance Faire and had been an active participant since the beginning. She had a booth at the faire and served her trifle and smoothies. This meant being gone over the weekends for seven weeks. She would leave on Friday afternoon and get back on Sunday night leaving me alone at the house.

On one such Saturday morning, I was up early when noticed a car pull up with and woman inside the car. She stopped, reached over and picked up a baby and proceeded to get out of the car. Another car pulled up and a silvered-haired man got out of the car and met her. Then they both came to my door. I reluctantly opened the door, not knowing either one of these people. But they did look familiar. I opened the door and they both stood there. I asked them if I could help them? The man who looked like David Jacobs said to me, "Come on Steve, you know who I am you read all of my books. The woman looked like one of Gilly's best friends. But I knew it wasn't her. And this wasn't David Jacobs. I was a little unsettled with all of this and suddenly they pushed past me, came into the house and took charge of me. Somehow they had this power over me I couldn't resist and they took me into the bedroom laid me face down on the bed and removed my robe and nightshirt. I remember the woman placing her hands on my back. I couldn't move and I could hear them talking back and forth but I couldn't make it out clearly. Then she placed her hands on my back. I felt this incredible warmth, a loving warm come from her hands and flow throughout my body and I became unconscious. When I came to, I found myself still face down on the bed with my robe pulled down. I was groggy and a bit disoriented. I wondered if I had just fallen asleep that way and it was all just a dream. So I went into the bathroom and took a look at my back. What I found was two areas on my back that were red right where her hands had been placed. I went to the front and looked out the windows but they were gone. I thought about what might have happened for a long time. I felt that whoever did this appeared as people I knew and with whom I would trust and feel comfortable. It's true I read David Jacobs book, "Secret Life" but I didn't read all of them. And the woman was a friend of Gilly's I had always been attracted too. I read before and heard of other peoples' experiences with this screening and appearing to be people you trusted and or loved. Dr. Karla Turner (who was a friend) often talked about the visitors ability to project images to have control over you. I couldn't remember beyond them coming into the house and taking control of me what happened next.

Chapter Twenty-Eight

Another World

Another Faire weekend, in the morning, there was a knock on the door. I looked out the front window and could see a city water and power truck parked there. I figured they wanted to tell me they would be turning off the power or water for a while to do a repair. I opened the door and two men stood there in hard hats. One was black and the other Caucasian. They smiled and I asked if I could help, to which the black man held up a small credit card sized device that had a flat screen embedded in it. This is something we didn't have in the nineties. He said to me, "Come on Steve, you know who we are; it's time to go". I looked to my right at the truck and what I saw looked like an Airstream trailer except it was round like an aircraft fuselage. It was hovering off the ground. What happened next, I remembered. We went out to the silver metal vehicle and they put me onboard. Inside was much, like an airliner with rows of seats and people sitting in them. They were unconscious. They sat me in one of the seats and I fell asleep. Later I woke up and looked around. There was a tall man in a suit standing in the isle. He was tall and human looking but different somehow. I got up and walked over to him. I stopped and looked around. And this is when I noticed the porthole windows. I told him that this was brilliant. If anyone woke up they'd just think they were on a plane. He just smiled at me. "That's right," he said not moving his mouth. He then asked me to get back in my seat. I asked him why I was awake when the others were not. He told me the same thing. You are different, special. How many times have I heard this? Why always the same line? So then I'm sitting in my seat and I'm looking out the widow and below me is the most beautiful world I have ever seen. It was like something out of a fantasy. It was green and lush everywhere and the architecture blended with the environment. We were descending and soon reached the ground. A door opened up on the vehicle and I got up and walked toward it. The tall strange man was there and gestures towards the open door and told me to exit and enjoy. Enjoy? This was so different than anything I had experienced up to this point. I felt like I was on a field trip. When I got outside it hit me. This had to be heaven and I just died. Maybe not, but the air here was like being in a pine forest. It was totally lacking in pollution of any kind. The sense of wellbeing was if everything that had ever been a burden to your soul was lifted and gone. The weight of the world was gone, the stress, the sadness. All I could feel was total absolute joy. I walked into park, and, looking around as far as I could see, this entire world was like one big beautiful park. There were lots of people of all sizes and shapes. One very strange looking man, sitting under a tree, caught my eye. The man was relaxing in the shade. I walked over to him to get a better look. He was humanoid, wearing a suit and a hat. This was been another reoccurring scene in my experience. The brim was down a bit casting a shadow on his face. His face was covered with a fine covering of thin hair. It was thin enough that I could see his skin through it and the color was a pale grey. "You're not from around here," I asked. He looked up at me pushing the brim back and smiled. His eyes were larger than most humans and they were dark. Not black but dark and I could see he had enlarged irises and pupils with very pale white barely visible. "It is you that is not from here", he replied. Stupidly I asked him if he was an alien and he told me that we were all the same but only looked different physically. "We all come here to rest and take a pause in our lives and to reflect on our existence." I looked down and saw the hoofed feet my grandfather had once described to me. I wondered if this was he. Was he an old friend and not the devil himself? Although the feet looked like hooves they could have been shoes and had the look of hooves. He tipped his head down again to rest under the tree giving me a passing smile as he did. Despite his rather odd appearance, I felt nothing but love and joy from this being that may have scared my grandfather so long ago. I looked around the park and saw many people relaxing there. Some looked just like humans. Others were different. In some cases they were very different.

There were benches with couples sitting and engaged in conversation. It was then that I remembered sitting on one of these benches with my Dad, after he had passed away. He came to tell me he loved me and that he was fine. I remembered this and wondered were all these people doing the same thing? Were they talking and sharing a last moment with someone they loved now that they passed on? It was at this point I started to under-stand that the world of the Visitors and the alleged dead were connected. And that the Visitor's world was mine too. I am part of it myself. I am also a visi-tor. At that moment I felt a calm I had never experi-enced before.

I found a tree and sat under it. I looked up at the sky, breathed the air and watched the silver cigar - shaped vehicles silently pass over. I would visit this place again and again. And only, now as I write this, am I becoming increasingly aware of what this place means and why I feel such peace here. In writing this book, it too is part of my journey, my exploration and discovery.

Chapter Twenty-Nine

Further Contacts

All during this period the experiences and contacts were at an all-time high. It seemed sometimes daily, and in talking to other experiencers, I found it to be happening to them too. At the CERO support groups it was apparent.

One evening I was taking out the trash. It was a clear night and a bit windy. I went to the alley, on the side of our house, and got the trashcan. I rolled it and opened the gate that leads to the front yard and the street. I place the trashcan on the street. I turned around to head back when two small Asian women approached me. They were quite small and they were wearing white shirts with dark ties and pants. They had bobbed haircuts shoulder length. Their hair was dark. They stopped and started talking to me in what I thought at the time, Chinese. Upon further reflection, it wasn't that at all; it was completely foreign. I thought that maybe they were lost and were looking for another address, as we did have Asian neighbors nearby. I told them I couldn't understand them and to try next door. Feeling a bit uneasy, I walked back to the gate and went inside the alley and closed it. I looked over the gate to see what they were doing, only to find them just standing there starring at me. It was at this moment I sensed a calm. The wind had stopped. I turned around to go back in the house through the side entrance when I saw a light in the sky. It was getting closer and, as it did, it looked like a flying car. It had lights on it and some on the bottom that looked like colored neon. We had this huge Chumash tree and as it came over the tree and directly over me and stopped. I opened the door to the house and started to go in, never taking my eyes off the object; when suddenly this soft blue white beam appeared. I have to admit that I was a little unsettled. I looked at the beam and knew it was for me. I was wide-awake and knew I wasn't dreaming. I kept looking at the beam and I understood. Walk into it. So I did. My heart was in my throat but I did it. As I did, I felt weightless and I started to float upwards. The next thing I can remember is being in a dimly lit building. It was barren with hallways and adjoining rooms through doorways. A very tall thin man was leading me. Much like the ones I had met before, but no hats this time. He had some kind of jumpsuit on. I asked him, "Where are we going?" and he said, "A place you want to see. ". He took me into a large, open room that had a long table and some chairs. The lights were off. It was dark and there was this large window with a soft light coming lighting the floor and the room. The man took me over to the window, and as he did, I could see stars, lots of stars. There were more stars than I had ever seen before. As I stood at the window, I leaned into the recessed window frame and looked around. Then I saw it. To my right I could see the curve of the Earth from space. I could also see this large faceted struc-ture. I could only imagine that it must have been the outside of a large spacecraft. I looked back at the being. He smiled and said, "Stay here for awhile and enjoy this gift. We know how much it means to you." He walked away and went out thought a door into the hallway. I stayed there just staring out at the stars. It seemed like an hour. I never wanted it to end. All my life I had always wanted to go into space and here I was. I never wanted to let it go. I started to cry with joy. Then I felt a hand on my shoulder. I was told it was time to go. We left the room and walked down the hallway. The next thing I remembered was being in the back seat of this flying vehicle. It was dark inside and pretty drab. No flashing lights or knobs. There was a man sitting in the front in one of two seats. I could see between them and there was this ball that looked iron-colored, old and very used. He had his hand on it and suddenly I felt movement. The window next to me revealed that we were moving through some sort of tunnel. I kept watching and, as I did, we left the tunnel and we were in space. I could see part of the huge ship. It soon moved out-of-view, as we turned and descended towards the Earth.

It wasn't long before we were over my house. I was looking down at it. The next thing I knew I woke up on my coach in the shop. It was cold and I still had my coat one. The side door was open and the wind was blowing a cold Santa Ana. I got up to close it and looked up at the stars. I closed the door and went inside. Gilly was asleep so I sneaked into bed and went to sleep.

Chapter Thirty
Whitley Strieber

I always wanted to meet Whitley Strieber, ever since I read his book, <u>Communion</u>. I made a new friend, who was a writer for comic books, and he too had these experiences. We worked together to do some prototypes for a new Comic called, <u>Beyond Communion</u> and Whitley was involved. Martin had put a deal together with *Caliber Comics* He had recently met with Whitley to do a series of comics based <u>Communion</u>.

One night the phone rang late and I picked it up. It was Whitley Strieber. It was one of those amazing moments in one's life. We talked for over an hour about the experience, the comic and the art he would need for the covers. Up to this point, I had made three prototype versions that I illustrated myself. But in the end I would be making the covers. This began a long friendship that remains to this day.

He and Anne would often pop into town and drop by my house and we'd go out to dinner and chew the fat. I eventually would appear on TV shows with him and at conventions. I was able to introduce him to another friend of mine, Dr. Roger Leir who I had met at a MUFON meeting in Newbury Park. This then lead to us sharing an amazing experience in attending some of the first implant-removal surgeries.

Dr. Roger Leir was a man who took an interest in the field of close encounters research back in the early nineties. I originally met him at a MUFON (The Mutual UFO Network) meeting in Newbury Park, California, where we became friends. We worked together on cases and investigations but when I met Whitley, I just had to hook the two of them up together. It wasn't long before Whitley and I attended one of the Dr. Leir's first implant-removal surgeries. This was difficult for Whitley. He felt this sense of a disturbance, as if the implant wasn't to be removed. It was an implant located in a woman's toe. She had close encounters all her life. It was an amazing event. A near first with the exception of a friend, Jesse Long who had one removed some years before.

In all cases I would come to know, the implants were not something that could be explained away as "one of those things". They were made of meteoric materials and had human nerve cells growing out of metal material. They sometimes would give off radio signals. Later we would fine that some were laced with nanotubes. In all the cases there were no entry scars.

I could go on a length about this subject but there has been so many good research books written about this subject, (many by Roger Leir) that there is no need for me to continue on about it here.

Whitley, Roger and I appeared on the "Alien Interview" that Bob Kiviat produced of an alleged tape smuggled out of *Area 51* that showed a gray being interrogated.

I introduced Whitley to Yvonne Smith and many of the folks at the local MUFON group in Southern California.

Whitley would talk for hours about all of this. And he has helped me on so many occasions in my life. I started having so many problems just keeping employed with the studios. Whitley and Anne started giving me work that they needed done. I created book covers, videos and illustrations for them. He also allowed me the rights to produce busts and a full-sized wearable mask of the *Communion* lady from the famous book cover. I also made T-Shirts. I could never thank him enough because he and Anne always included me when they could. He promoted my work on his web pages, TV shows and radio. He even wrote about me in his books. Best of all, Anne and Whitley are my friends. Anne was a joy to be around. She was genius in her wit and had the ability to really chew-the-fat with me on any subject.

Whitley, Anne and I were at this convention in the Bay Area in 1996. I had a booth at the Con and was a key speaker I talked about my experiences while showing my art. One night Anne and Whitley asked me up to their room for some wine and conversation. Their room had an upstairs bedroom loft that over looked the living room. Anne grew tired and said good night and went upstairs. Whitley and

I talked for some time then we both retired for the evening. One night we were coming back from Santa Barbara, after attending a lecture we were invited to by Michael Lindeman. Whitley was driving us back to LA late at night. Anne was in the back seat and told the story of how she marveled at the two of us (that night at the convention in the bay area) as she watched us both from the upstairs loft. She told us both, as she recounted the evening, how amazing it was to watch this longhaired rock-and-roller guy sharing conversation with her rather straight-looking husband. She laughed, as she talked about it, as we were indeed an odd couple. She thought it was a wonderful moment, to watch us both enjoy each other's company, as well as we did. I have never forgotten that. Then I said something about a big bug. Whitley was silent for a moment and then said, "Big Bug, sounds like a band" and we all had a good laugh.

Whitley would later be there for one of the most life-changing experiences I would ever journey through. He would be there for me as I later would be for him, as he would soon experience the same.

Chapter Thirty-One

The Kitchen Visit

One of those most striking encounters I ever had was late one night at the Granada Hills house. I woke up around 3:00 a.m., again. On this night, I was thirsty and headed out to the kitchen to get some water from the refrigerator. I was a bit sleepy still and walked along, while looking down at the floor, when I arrived at the kitchen. It was dimly lighted with night-lights Gilly had all over the house. As I got to the refrigerator, I saw that Gilly had left the butcher table in the middle of the kitchen floor. It was blocking the refrigerator. I was perplexed. Why would she do this? My mind had automatically gone to the first plausible explanation: the wooden legs of a table. In that moment, I saw what I thought were the legs to the cutting board move. And get this: there were only two tan legs not four. In an instant I knew what was happening. The legs were thin and featureless with hoof-like feet. I looked up from the feet to the body and head. There before me was this tiny little being with black eyes and a smile on her face. We had a moment where we had gazed into one another eyes. I had a connection and so much went through my mind in an instant. She was an old friend. Then, in a flash, she moved so fast it was a blur; she went through the counter and wall. I ran to the living room to see if she was in there but it was dark and she was gone.

I felt, looking back, that I had caught her off-guard. But I could never be sure. I was wide-awake and fully conscious when this happened and it wouldn't be the last time.

Another time it happened, it was broad daylight, around noontime. I was in the workshop and I heard a noise on the side of the house. It sounded like someone working on the roof. We didn't have any work scheduled so I went outside to take a look. When I got outside, there was this man scraping the edges of the roof; peeling off the paint. He appeared to be in his forties, dark short hair with a pock-marked face. He was wearing a moth-eaten old sweatshirt and beat-up blue jeans. He wore no shoes.

It was about that time I noticed he wasn't sup-ported by a ladder of any kind but rather just floating in mid-air. Then it struck me. This is all wrong. He looked at me and said hello. I asked what he was doing and he said he just fixing the roof. I told him we didn't have anyone working on the roof. Seeing him floating there I called out. "Hey you're an Alien!" At that moment he dropped down from the roof and faced me. He morphed into the Visitor lady. This time it was a taller version but the same sort of tan skin and black eyes. In fact, she looked just like the cover of Whitley's famous book. She held up a finger to me and waved it from side to side. She gave me this smile and, it was at that point, I thought I saw what looked like teeth. She moved back from me and started moving towards the gate. In a blur, she shot through the gate. As I ran to the gate and looked over it, she was in the street. She spun in a circle so fast she looked like a sandy dust devil and vanished.

Chapter Thirty-Two

Dr. Roger Leir and My Implant

I met Roger in 1995 at a MUFON meeting in Newbury Park, California. We hit it off immediately, as we both had a passion for the subject. Roger originally started off as a skeptic, however the claim that experiencers made about having implants, caught his attention. If you have an implant, he wanted to see it and study it. He thought the best way to study the implants was to remove one and see if it could be explained or identified as unknown. He removed many. I often attended the surgeries. He was a friend and always invited me.

I had, for some time, been noticing a raised area on my right forearm. It is just under the epidermis and could easily be removed. It was perfectly round and not very thick. I showed this to Roger and he wanted to take a closer look. He invited me out to Thousand Oaks to have an X-ray; I agreed. This would turn out to be an amazing event for me. Roger met me and the X-ray tech took the x-ray of my arm. Roger had to leave early and could wait to see the results, so I stayed while the x-ray tech developed the film. He came out from the lab and hung the large x-ray up on the light table. We couldn't see much just a slight outline of the object that appeared nearly transparent. We could just make it out. The real subject of this x-ray would turn out to be something unexpected.

The tech asked me how I broke my arm and I must have been in a great deal of pain. He pointed at a perfectly thin black line running at a 45-degree angle across both the bones in my forearm. I told him I had never broken a bone in my life and I could not account for the dark line. He told me that he has been an x-ray tech for a long time and knew a bad break when he saw one. But I argued that I had never broken my arm. This annoyed him so much he told me I was lying to him. He then asked me to leave. I told him again I was telling the truth but he didn't believe me.

I left the office and went to my car where things got interesting. I drove a 1985 Nissan 300zx. It had T-tops that were made in glass. As I got in my seat, I looked up and the streetlight directly over me went out. This has happened before, many times. In fact, it's well known in this field, that this will often happen to experiencers. But on this night, it would be more than I could ever imagine. As I drove out of the parking lot, light after light I passed under went out. It was eerie. I got on to the 23 Highway towards Granada Hills and whole banks of streetlights were going out as I drove down the highway. It didn't stop until I got home and pulled in the driveway. It never happened quite like that again. I will never know why this happens and, until this day, it can still occur. This night, something was different. I made a discovery that night. The broken arm appeared surgical in every way. I was totally unaware of the break. There is a thin line in the same location on both my arms that has the appearance of an old scar, very thin, but very there. It was as if both arms had been removed and put back but I'll never know for sure. For years I tried to get the x-ray from Roger but sadly he died before I could. I plan to have both arms x-rayed. I don't know if I will be able to get them from Roger's family, who are holding on to them. He was also my podiatrist and doctor.

In talking to Whitley, he tells me he had something similar with his neck; a surgery had been done that he can't remember. He also told me that we weren't alone in this. Others have also reported the same.

I last saw Roger at my studio in Ventura two weeks before he passed. He came to visit and he needed help with a video. I'm glad I had this last opportunity to spend some time with my dear friend. I miss being able to call him up and talk to him. He was always there for me and for all of us for whom he cared so deeply. He was a good man and a good friend.

Chapter Thirty

Three: Rough Days Ahead

I eventually decided not to have the implant removed. The harassment we were having continued as did the experiences. Gilly and I were being stalked and followed. Black helicopters were always around the house and phones bugged.

All during this time, I continued my work at the conferences and on television, discussing my experiences and presenting my evidence. I had just interviewed with the studios for another contract to build alien creatures for a feature film. I got the job and Gilly and I were very happy about it. I started getting emails about this time that claimed they were CIA and NSA. They warned me that my talking to the public was breaking my contract with them and not to speak about it. If I did not stop soon, it could be unpleasant for me. I showed these emails to Jeff Rense, Whitley and others and their opinions varied. Most thought it was a hoax. I wasn't sure myself, but didn't treat it lightly. This had happened to others and things went very wrong for them. I was now worried.

I was preparing for a job at the studio when I got a phone call from the producer with whom I had interviewed. I was happy to hear from her and she wanted to ask me a question. I thought it would be about the movie project but instead, to my shock, she asked me if I'm in trouble with the law. I was perplexed to say the least! I told her emphatically no, I wasn't in any way in trouble with the law. She told me that I had to be in some kind of trouble because two men came to their office in an official capacity and warned the studio that I was trouble. They told her that it wasn't in their best interest to work with me. Needless to say, I protested but to no avail as I lost the job.

My wife was petrified. Who would do this? I asked the producer who they were, but like the post office, she said she couldn't help me. Now I was beginning to question should I stop and go silent? Or should I fight? Again my friends believed that it was a very bad prank. I wasn't sure and continued on. As I did, the harassment got worse and continued.

It was right about this time that I got a call from Dr. Roger Leir about a sighting in Camarillo, California. And this would be the last public investigation of UFO's for me.

Chapter Thirty-Four

Camarillo UFO

In 1998 I got a call from Roger about the Camarillo UFO. It has been sighted before in November. Many had seen it and it came to Roger's attention by reports to MUFON. Roger knew I was an amateur astronomer and that I also had an 8-inch Celestron Telescope with a 2000mm scope on an equatorial mount and clock drive. He described the UFO, as he had gone out to see it himself. It would appear right after sunset, in the twilight coming out of the northwest, with consistency. I wondered if it were just a star or planet but the direction wasn't right for a planet. The following evening I went out and met Roger and some of the MUFON members with only a pair of binoculars. I wanted a look first before I brought out all the heavy equipment.

When I first saw it, it was coming up from the northern horizon. It was moving much like a satellite. The object had a blue color to it. I looked through the binoculars and what I saw was not a satellite. It was a hat-shaped saucer, a classic UFO. We watched it for a long time. It continued its trajectory until, off over the trees; we could no longer see it. That was enough for me. It wasn't a star or a satellite.

I went home that night and made a camera mount for a Sony 8mm video camera I had. I still have that mount to this day. I put it together with aluminum I got from Home Depot and pop rivets. I used prime focus through a 1.4 mm eyepiece. It worked quite well for what it was, however under extreme magnification, it was difficult to keep any object or star tracked well. It was the best I had. The following night I went to the sight and set everything up. Roger was there and the rest of the group that were there the night before. I set up a monitor and connected it to the camera feed so everyone could see the object.

Like clockwork, it appeared. It looked the same and I quickly got it in the finder scope and centered in the eyepiece. This time it was different. It was a large sphere and extending from it was what I could only describe as an energy beam. At the end of this beam was a bright light and the whole object moved in a pendulum motion. The motion was from side to side. It did this for a long time and I kept following it; hand tracking all the way. Then suddenly, it exploded in a perfect circle, and emitted smaller saucer shaped lights from it. They slowly moved away until we could no longer see them. I captured the whole event on video. None of us knew exactly what we had seen. It was very exciting to say the least. I wondered if it was something we had in space. But if it was, it was quite large. We didn't have ISS yet or anything else like it that we knew.

I went home pretty excited and studied it for hours. I loaded it to my website and shared it with the public. Many thought it was just a weather balloon that was swinging from a tether. It didn't look like that at all. It is doubtful a weather balloon would show up consistently every night in the same location.

Whitley later had the video analyzed, as did Roger Leir. Both reports came back labeled as an unknown. The video is still available to watch online.

This video started even more trouble for me. The harassment escalated. "You weren't supposed to talk about this," I was told. By now this was all starting to be harder and harder on my family and career. I wasn't getting work from the studios and my career was hurting. I had to decide what to do next.

Chapter Thirty-Five

Steve Neill Walks

By May of 1999, I had had quite enough. Things had reached a zenith. I had to put an end to all this. Whoever had put so much pressure on me, whether it was the Government or some other entity had to quit this harassment. My wife had been pleading with me to quit. In fact she threatened to leave me if I didn't. It was time.

I had made friends with a radio show host named Jeff Rense. He was, one of many, who had appeared on talk shows with me. I had written a letter to the UFO community at large. I was very well known among the enthusiasts and colleagues of the UFO field. I knew I had to make a big noise to be heard and hopefully reaching the ears of those that were harassing me. Jeff reviewed the letter and edited it and released it on his web site. To this day, you can still read the letter, if you do the search, "Steve Neill Walks".

I see things differently today but keep in mind I was trying to lose the bad guys from my life. In reading it today, I can truthfully say I don't agree with everything I had said. I wrote this letter 18 years ago.

Here is a copy of the letter:

5-15-99

After being involved in the most serious UFO research and direct experiences with ET all my life, the behavior of most of the UFO community has become such a disgrace, so vile and demented, that I have decided to withdraw from the field permanently.

All the petty, infantile mudslinging and politics, the backstabbing and throat-slitting, the egos and the liars, the radio cult figures, the betrayal of 'friendships' have all overshadowed the critical issues at hand...and have often made virtual laughing stock of anyone who innocently tries to tell the truth.

The UFO 'community' is its own worst enemy. Any respect this field might have had or been due to receive has been destroyed by the actions of many, if not most, of the key players involved. I say *most* involved because there are some very good professional people in the field...but they are a relative few and maintain low profiles for the most part.

After many, many years of involvement and serious study, I have regrettably had to accept that many of the good people who come into contact with this subject are often destroyed by it, and can lose family, friends and even their careers because

189

of the fighting and manipulation and treachery running rampant.

Perhaps the people who designed and implemented the 50-year UFO cover-up are right. Perhaps they know exactly what they were -and are - doing. Perhaps they realized it by simply watching the behavior of the UFO 'community' and knew better than to give this biggest secret of all to the masses. Without doubt, if the world at-large acted like the UFO 'community'...the world might well stop...the engine of society gagging itself to a dead stall after choking on the outrageous lies, deceit, fraud, hate, and hoaxes that so permeate the UFO 'culture' these days.

In retrospect, perhaps some of my own actions have been Irresponsible and may have unwittingly contributed to the stress and downfall of some...in the sense that my experiences terrified them and set up an opportunity for hustlers to play on the underlying current of exaggeration, fear, and anxiety that hearing these experiences can bring about. Somewhat naively, I thought it was important that people know and that it might help some of them. But for all those I helped, I may have done service to many more.

It can be reckless to alarm the public, even if you do have proof. We should think more of what the 'truth' could do to those who hear it...instead of what it can do for we who know.

This isn't a warning about pollution or some social injustice but of an invasion by beings from another world(s) who have*total control* over us. And we, as a species, haven't a clue.

That kind of knowledge can destroy one's ambition, social parameters, and, in some extreme cases, even the will to live.

This we cannot allow to happen. Certainly, many humans may be 'ready' for the 'truth' but given the current state of the world...and the strangle hold on over half the world's population by organized 'religion'...the results would be catastrophic.

Finally, it would be a much better use of our time if we pursued issues we CAN control in order to provide a real future for our children...those who can still think for themselves.

Have any of you talked to a 16 year old lately? Many of our own children, tomorrow's 'leaders,' have very little hope for the future. They often live for the moment and the next high (drugs or otherwise) and their heroes are all too often dark' movements,' and dark rock bands with their dark and ugly lyrics, dark video games of death and terror, and dark thought which is spawned and nurtured in their young minds by the greed-obsessed 'entertainment' industry and other mass-mind control mechanisms. What happened to the The Beatles and John Glenn? What happened to at least the idea of morals and positive values? Responsibility? Accountability? What happened to the concept of 'giving'?

The same egomania and self-aggrandizement that fuels the morons who top the pop music charts is found in the UFO 'community' as well. Oh yes, the vocabulary is a little more astute but don't kid yourself, it's the same old rocket-to-stardom "I wanna be a star" syndrome.

In the UFO 'community' theft of others' research has replaced the real thing. Many 'researchers' go to conferences and on radio programs and simply spew various mixtures of other peoples' data...begged, borrowed, and just plain stolen. When is the last time you heard someone unique...who actually said something 'new'? It doesn't happen very often.

It's time to try to reach back to being the great beings we were...and are...so that we may reach ahead and make it to that future which holds so much promise. We went to the Moon over 30years ago and what a proud moment it was.

Now it's time to journey to Mars...and the stars beyond...where one day WE will become the aliens. Let's give the world something positive for a change. For starters, let's stop knocking NASA. Sure, every agency has its problems but overall they've done more to help this planet and its people than any of you UFO folks will ever hope to do. It's stupid to make an enemy out of the very people who have the keys to our own Starship.

I know some of you will be offended by my actions and my words. You wouldn't expect it from

Steve Neill of all people. Well, it's time to wake up and smell the coffee; you don't know 10% of what you think you do. After all, there is life after UFOs and it's a great one I plan on living. My efforts at this point are to shift back to what I was doing before all this started...to promoting manned space explora-tion anyway I can. You will already see examples of this redirected energy on my website and there will be more to come.

All the Universe or Nothingness.

The choice is ours.

After the letter was released, I got a deluge of email asking me to hang in there. I was told that I was a valuable contributor to the field. They brought up that my artwork would be missed. Please at least continue on with the art. But I didn't.

It was Christmas 1999.We were having our popular Christmas Day party with our many friends. One of them was a woman named Licia Davidson. She had many dramatic encounters with both the Visitors and the Feds. We had a lot in common, however unlike me, she actually pursued her human abductors and the helicopters to the point of danger. She asked me that night, what I was going to do with all the artwork and sculptures I had done over the years. My art was lined up in my office and I just could not bring myself to look at it anymore. So I gave her all my original art and sculptures as a

Christmas present. She had helped me a lot during my rough period. She helped me by her listening and she helped me with money by generously offering to help. Work wasn't coming in anymore and she knew why. The least I could do was give her my art that she loved so much. She loaded up her suburban and took it all away. Even the gray alien puppets I did for the TV shows such as "Sightings" and "Paranormal Borderline". They were all gone. Nothing remained. She took a burden from me. Time would tell what would happen next.

Jeff Rense called me one day to ask if I'd do a last show with him. I thought about it for a while and then agreed to do it. I assured Gilly this would be the last time. This would be the media send-off for me. I would be heard. It was now the beginning of the year in 2000. We had just moved to a new house up the street from the old one. I don't recall the date of the interview, but I did that last show with Jeff. We talked about the letter and my feelings on the subject. I told him, towards the end of the interview, that there would be some sort of response for my doing this. He asked me what I meant and I told him I'd get an email, or a strange phone call, or something like that from the Feds. We concluded the interview and we said our last goodbyes and I put the phone down.

Gilly was in the living room at the dining room table. She asked me how it went. I told her it was fine and we were all done. It was at that very moment the house shook a bit, and then a bit more. It was clearly a low-flying helicopter. It was right over the house. There were a floor-to-ceiling sliding glass doors that faced our backyard. I started to get up to go outside and Gilly asked me not too. But I did anyway. She put her head down and I opened the door and walked out. I went into the yard where I could still see Gilly sitting at the table. I looked up and, just over the house, maybe 200 foot up or less, was a large all *Sikorsky H-19* or something very similar. I could see the pilot who was wearing a white shirt and a dark tie. He had a white helmet on with the visor pulled down. He was just hovering there looking at me. I beckoned to Gilly to come out to see it. She did and when she saw it she said nothing. I saluted the pilot and he flashed a light at me and saluted back. With that he turned on his axis and slowly moved away off into the distance and was gone. That was the last time for them too. Everything stopped. I got one last email saying how smart it was of me to comply with their wishes and I never heard from them again. The phone stopped clicking, my mail flowed and all the harassment stopped. You could hear a pin drop.

The visits, still they occurred. And people around me were still aware of it.

Chapter Thirty-Six

The Years That Followed

I tried hard to get things back to normal, as best I could. I was lucky to get hired by a dot-com company in Sunnyvale, California. I worked remotely making computers images for an online chat social media sight.

This lasted for about a year and really helped me get back on my feet. We got the odd TV show here and there. I was learning a new trade in Lightwave 3D CGI that I hoped would keep me in work, since it was starting to replace practical effects work that I had done all those years. Things were good and then Silicone Valley had its big crash and I was one of the casualties. I lost my job and was on the hunt again. It wasn't too long after that that the owner of the home we were renting sold the house and we had to move out.

We moved to Northridge, California, just down the hill from our former home. I got some more movie work again just after we moved, building and flying radio controlled airplanes for a film. In fact, I continued getting more involved in the community of RC airplanes and scratch built and produced radio controlled jets for that community. It helped keep the rent and bills paid.

For a few more years I continued re-inventing myself by making model radio submarine kits, boat kits, and even model rockets. I was making income from things I loved and knew.

One day I was called by the "History Channel" to do some CGI work for a series called, "The UFO Files". It lead to more shows and this helped, despite the irony of it all. They knew of my own experience and ask me to be on the show. I declined.

Whitley also got me involved in his projects whenever he could to help us out. Again, it was an UFO abduction show called, "Alien Intent". I again was asked to appear and talk about my experience and declined. I just wanted to do their effects.

This went on for long time. All during this time, I was not without sightings and strange incursions. But they were far less. Still they were there. And so was the sound of the machine. I simply tried to not pay attention. I kept my ear to the field always and stayed in touch with Whitley, Yvonne, and Roger. But I stayed out of it. I did this mainly for the sake of my dear wife. I had told her no more. I stick to my promises.

One day Gilly went to the doctors for a breast exam and came home with the news that she had breast cancer. This was the beginning of a very long road that would eventually lead to her passing. She had a mastectomy of one breast. She was told she would need further treatment to make sure it was gone. The treatments were Chemo and radiation. Gilly refused both. For a few years there it looked like she'd be okay, as she thought it had not returned. She simply didn't believe in the treatments and felt she didn't need them. She was a very headstrong person; neither her daughter nor I could convince her otherwise. Ever since Gilly had the surgery, it was hard to get any real rest sleeping with her. She was up and down all night. She would wake up and turn the TV on, get up to make herself something in the kitchen, or just couldn't sleep. Gilly was on a lot of pain meds and sleep aids, which made her a zombie, for lack of a better description. Needless to say, it was a downward spiral.

One night, quite by surprise, I had another visit. I was sleeping in the bedroom next to our master bedroom. I awoke in my pajamas in the middle of our street standing under a streetlight. I could feel the rocks and gravel through my socks. I was disoriented and alarmed that the police might come by and ask me questions. I started back to the house when I noticed movement to my left and then, in a swoop, this small figure which reminded me of the grim reaper, came at me, wrapped itself around me and we started going straight up into the sky. I looked up to see the familiar black disc-shaped shadow and we went right into it. Once inside, I found myself in a corridor. It didn't look particular alien or strange, more like offices. The little figure with the hood was with me and took me to what looked like an office with frosted windows. Through the windows I could make out movement of people. I was taken in and there were very odd-looking tall humanoids. They were all standing around an examination table. They all looked at me and smiled.

They welcomed me in and told me to lie down. They told me they had a birthday present for me. It had just been my birthday, as a fact. I lied down on the table and they place a black rectangular box on my chest. I remember the box just sitting there and they all said happy birthday and this would help me. They seemed all so happy about it. Next thing I knew I sat up straight out of my bed. My heart was racing. I knew what just happened and it was a dream. I was emotional. It had been a long time and I worried I'd wake up Gilly. I left my room and stepped down t to the dark living room we had, I grabbed on to my beloved dog, Phooka and held on to her shaking. I didn't have another event like that for a few more years.

Gilly and I made a film for fun called "Foo Fighters". It was a WW2 movie about fighter pilots and their encounter with a UFO. This kept us going and we eventually finished it but could never sell the film, as we had hoped too. Still it was a good effort and a lot of fun to do.

I went on with my life as usual. When work didn't come in, I made my own. I always wanted a large model of the original Star Ship Enterprise. I decided to make one from scratch and eventually, due to its popularity on social media, it lead to contracts from collectors who wanted high-end models, like the Enterprise, in their collections. This lead to more and more projects that paid. I was starting to make a real living again but unknown to us, Gilly was getting sticker.

Gilly had been to the doctor a few times for some growths that appeared on her chest. The doctor thought it was shingles and started treating it. Time went on but it was getting worse. She went for a second opinion. I remember the day well. She came home and told me she had stage-4 breast cancer. I knew what that meant. Many around her, Gilly's daughter included, were in denial but I knew the end was near.

She started treatments at the City of Hope, futile though they were. Hope was the keyword. Keeping life normal from day to day for her was important. Giving up wasn't an option. I had hoped, just maybe, the treatments (which she should have had years ago) might work and we'd have a miracle. Gilly continued to get worse. I became her caretaker. I kept working around the clock and I attended to her. I had to keep working because the income I was bringing in was paying off the mounting bills, including the rent. I was there night and day. Her daughter and friends would bring her to treatments while I continued to work to pay the bills. Her friends did not understand that we still had bills. I did my best, between caring for Gilly and getting the work out. Others would drop by to visit but we had no help. I was getting work again and lots of it. She was happy about it and I set up my bedroom next to hers as a workshop so I could be nearby. Gilly's daughter was a career person in the film biz and would show up a couple times a day but really wasn't there when I needed her the most.

During that time, I did lots of models for my friend, Doug Drexler. I made a Time Machine from the famous movie. I brought it into the bedroom to show her. Gilly's face lit up when I turned The Time Machine on and advanced the lever forward and the dish turned and the lights blinked. I was always there for Gilly.

She soon stopped eating; and couldn't get out of bed without my help. I remember telling Whitley about this. Whitley, as I have said, was always there for me. We talked daily. When he heard she wasn't eating, he told me to prepare myself for the inevitable. Gilly was preparing to leave us.

I went to bed one night and woke up in that world that I spoke of, the one with the air of a mountain forest. The place that had a peace about it that I had never known and I had met the strange people and took a ride on the silver cigars.

I was just there. At first I thought I was dreaming but I took a deep breath and exhaled. I was breathing and smelling. I could feel the road under my feet. I was in a real place. The silver ships flew overhead without making a sound. The road I was walking on had other people walking by and passing me. I looked around at my beautiful surroundings and then it hit me. "I'm not on Earth". As I had this thought, a man in a hat passed me stopped then turned. He said, "No you're not". He had a transparent skin and I could see blood vessels and muscles. His eyes were strange and enlarged. I didn't feel any threat from him. In fact, I felt love and peace. He smiled and went on his way. I felt so good, exhilarated. I had been through months of stress and little sleep. I looked around and saw one of the landing stations for the silver cigar ships. There were a group of beautiful silver haired ladies there. I went over to them and had a closer look. I got some warm smiles from them. They were wearing uniforms like flight attendants and they all wore these down-turned wings pinned to their blazers. I smiled back and roamed this beautiful world. I wished I could stay there forever. After some time, I was asked to get on a ship and I returned home.

I woke in my bedroom. It was morning. I checked on Gilly and she seemed unconsciousness, as a result of the many drugs for her pain.

Phooka, our dog had passed in 2010. On New Year's Day, 2011 Gilly and I went to get little Rosie, our new puppy. Now it was late 2012, around November. I took her for a walk, as I always did in the morning. I felt the sun shine on my face and felt, despite all I was experiencing, this love. I had this glow in my heart from where I had just been. That everything would be okay, however I was soon to walk alone.

In February 2013 Gilly peacefully passed from this life. I was relieved that her suffering had ended. I had witnessed so much pain and suffering. Gilly was finally at peace. I kissed her one last time and I never saw her again. Gill will always remain in my heart. I just know she went to that place I had visited. She was there, at home and in peace.

Chapter Thirty-Seven: Mary

I continued to live at the Northridge house and kept working. Just before Gilly passed, I met a nice new friend we called "Uncle Ted". He originally contacted me to help with a project I was working; a full sized replica of Capt. Kirk's chair from the original Star Trek TV show. He had built one himself and wanted to help me upholster the seat. We became friends. He was one of those great human beings with whom you just loved to spend time. We worked on all kinds of projects together and had a great time doing them. When Gilly was passing, he was right there for me. He helped out around the place in immeasurable ways. Ted came to the house weekly and helped me work on builds and projects I was doing for customers.

I was in pretty bad shape though. Exhausted and stressed from being a caretaker and worse, I had a bad hernia. I had known about it for a while and there was nothing I could do because I had to work and take care of Gilly. The hernia was extended. My intestines were popped out and all I could do was a patch. I pushed them back in and wore a truss. I wore that truss for six months or more. If it wasn't for Ted, I could never have gotten the things I needed done around the house. I didn't have any help beyond Uncle Ted and a few of my friends from the modeling and effects community. Doug Drexler helped me a bunch. Jeff Helps, whom I met online, came all the way from Canada to help me and give me comfort.

After Gilly passed, I rarely saw her daughter or long-time family friends except when they came and stripped property from our home during my grieving. They just stripped the place of things they thought were Gilly's as if we weren't married for over thirty years. They even took gifts that Gilly had bought me. I didn't have to let it happen I just did. Because when one has a loss like I just had, material things just seem inconsequential. I was in a daze and didn't realize what they were doing until later. I never saw any of them again even after knowing many of them for over 30 years. It was sad.

Ted, Doug, Whitley, Jeff and many of my newer friends I met through the modeling community were there. Shawn and her boy friend Robert helped too. I'll never forget them for that.

It was in April that I got a call from my old friend Tony. He asked me how I was doing. He wanted to know what's next for me. I told him I was just going to keep working on things I loved doing until I dropped. (I still had that hernia to deal with.) He asked if I was ever going to date again. It was too soon to tell and besides that I felt I was too old for that. Didn't even know where one would start.

Tony told me about a dating sight he frequented. Not for romance so much as just to have a girl friend, someone to talk with and have the pleasure of knowing. He said maybe I'd meet a friend there and it might help. I chuckled about it, thinking at the time, it was kind of a goofy idea. But I did think about it. I really didn't have girlfriends anymore.

I loved Gilly dearly, however, one thing that always really bothered me about her was her extreme jealousy. When I first moved in with her I started to notice it. It wasn't so obvious at first but, as time went by, it got worse. She was so uncomfortable with my talking or spending anytime with old girl friends, ones I had a relationship or were just friends. I had a picture in one of my books; a paperback of "Westworld" and inside I kept a picture of Judy. Judy was the girl that passed away on me suddenly. One day I went to get the picture and it was gone. I knew I left it there, so where was it. I asked Gilly about it and she became very angry claiming that she didn't know it was there or nor had she removed it. There were other pictures too that disappeared. It was so bad that after we were married, if a pretty woman passed me and I dared to look at her she would call me on it. I gave it a lot of thought.

Back to that dating site: I had waited a couple of weeks before I decided to take a look at it. One night, after a couple of glasses of wine, I went there, filled out a profile and waited to see what would happen. I was contacted by a few of the women. Most of the women wanted me to take care of them. Some just wanted a one-night-stand. None just wanted to have a date and talk.

I was about to give up when one night I checked my email and I had a 97 percent match to my profile. I went to the woman's profile and the first thing I saw was a beautiful woman. She had in her eyes a fire that breathed life. It was literally love at first sight. I sent her a message on the site. I told her about what I had just been through. I also told her she was beautiful, special and I just wanted her to know that. I didn't really expect to hear back from her and went on about my business. But the next day I did hear back from her.

She explained to me that she had just lost her husband to cancer a year ago and very much understood what I must have been feeling. She told me if I ever just needed someone to talk with, to call her and gave me her phone number. I called her with a lump in my throat and got her message service. I left a message and the next day she called me back. I remember Ted was there and he had this look on his face when I got the call, like a cat that just swallowed a canary. We talked for a long time. She told me all about her husband and asked about Gilly.

It wasn't too long after that we started using Skype and we met every night and became friends. Eventually I came up to her home in Port Hueneme and we had our first date. We dated a lot and fell in love.

I continued to live in Northridge and would spend the weekends with Mary. It was becoming increasingly clear that I had to deal with the hernia. Mary set out on finding me a good doctor to do the necessary surgery and found The Hernia Center of Southern California in Pasadena. I had the surgery at the end of May 2013. I thought I only had one, but they found five! Lifting during Gilly's care caused the hernias. Well, he patched me up and I stayed at Mary's for the weekend to heal before returning home to Northridge. In June we discussed getting out of Northridge and my moving up to Port Hueneme. I started making my plans to leave and started packing slowly but surely. We also decided to rent a studio where we could work in together. I was trying to work out of her place on weekends and it was becoming clear I needed more the space.

We found the ideal space in Ventura for the studio and not far from Mary's home, about 15 minutes. It then became SNG Studio. SNG stood for Steve Neill's Garage, a name Doug Drexler coined before I met Mary for the title of my popular YouTube channel. On July 7, 2013, we moved into the studio and I moved in with Mary. I never looked back. I was and still am in love with Mary.

Mary is an artist herself, a great painter and a creative and brilliant person. The studio does well and I continued to get modeling building work and other projects with prosthetics and creatures. But I still thought about filmmaking. It was my first love and the reason I came to Hollywood.

I told Mary early on in our relationship about the Visitors. She has interest astronomy, science and UFOs. She met and became friends with Whitley and Anne. We would visit with them and have great conversations about these subjects.

I can't remember when it was exactly, but Mary and I were driving home from the studio at night on Harbor Blvd, a two-lane road along the beach. Port Hueneme and Ventura are coastal towns. The road was dark and, as we drove along, we would often look at the sky and notice the objects in it.

One evening on that road, we saw this object coming towards us. At first we both thought it was a plane. But as it got closer, it was lacking in any FAA required NAV lights or strobes. As it got even closer, we could see its shape. It was a large triangle. Slowly it passed over us; then flew out over the ocean and was gone. This was our first sighting together and it wouldn't be our last. We have and still do to this day, see UFOs. Odd things happen in the house. Spoons would bend, screws back out of the cabinets, and knocks on the walls in threes and the ever-present hum that Mary can hear herself.

Many times we have been out with our interns or friends and we have been witness to UFOs .Two times it was our interns that pointed them out to us. The presence of the Visitors is always near. But Mary and I have always been comfortable with this knowledge.

I just wanted to make a short film again and have fun with filmmaking. We have a great time doing it. We have learned a lot of things and it led to me writing a full feature script that is looking for funding, as we I write this. Over the next three years, we would work on many projects at the studio. We made a short film called "Martians Attack SNG".

We started talking about making a dramatic series about my life with this experience. We would keep it simple and finance it ourselves to avoid the usual problems associated with taking on funding.

Chapter Thirty-Eight
But Something is There, The Pilot

I have made movies before where the "money people" completely changed the concept of the initial script. They had the money ergo; they had the control. I could not allow my work to be compromised this time. I have seen it too much. This time I would not accept money from anyone.

A good example of this for one is Travis Walton's "Fire in the Sky". It was a great book and we all know that Travis was telling the truth. Along comes Hollywood looking for material and they find Travis's story and want to turn it into a movie. The moment I heard this, I knew what they would do; and they did it. Changed the story to suit their audience and bring in the dollars. They changed everything, from the time the light hit him and he was taken on board. They turned it into a nightmare with hellish scary monsters with slim. Nothing about the abduction sequence was remotely like his accounting in his book.

I was at a MUFON meeting in the LA valley back at the time when the movie was released. Tracy Torme (the screen writer) was speaking there about his writing of the script for "Fire in the Sky". I listened both to him and the audience's questions. They were all starry-eyed over Tome. He pontificated at length about the film and how good it was. I could not take it anymore and raised my hand. To my surprise, he called me by name. Tracy was definitely someone who was interested in the visitors, but he was also a Hollywood writer and subject to the whims of that culture that I often resisted. I asked him the big question, "Why did you change Travis's version of the abductions? It was nothing like the book." Tracy was clearly annoyed by this question and rolled his eyes at me. It was clear that he was asked this before and he knew that this would happen. He told me, and I quote, "Steve what would you have me do? The producers told me if they saw those black eyed aliens one more time, we didn't have a picture and I'd be out of a job". My response was simple. I knew his job was at stake. However, what I said was true. "Tracy, they didn't have black eyes." It's true anyone that read the book would know this. He must have, but the producers never did. It was clear by the statement about the black eyes. To them, Travis was just another nut with a tall tale. They gave him no respect. I got a glare from the audience. Some gave me the thumbs up though, they had read Travis's book. This is a clear case for not accepting funding for a project like this. I could cite others, but if you are reading this book, then you know already know.

I wanted to portray this experience as it happened. Respect must be paid to the millions who have this experience. We must not spice it up with Hollywood WAM and POW. The subject doesn't need it; it takes away from all credibility.

I wrote a script. Mary edited it. We worked closely together. Whitley also assisted in reading the script and commented on his dialogue for the opening monologue. We asked him to host the show and introduce the story.

It was a good script and encompassed a lot of material. It gives the first-time viewer a broad spectrum of events that they could expect to see in future episodes. Our biggest problem was the title. Everything we came up with was taken. We were at our wits end when I got a call from Whitley. He was going to be speaking at Leigh McCloskey's home in Malibu. We were happy to attend to hear Whitley's Talk. He talked a long time about his experience, the Visitors and the conflict he had faced from the public, who had labeled him an "Alien cult leader" on more than one occasion. Anyone who knows Whitley knows this is the furthest thing from the truth. He said that, in all his experience, no one really knows for sure what this contact origin and identity is. But he went on to say, "But Something is There." At that moment Mary and I turned to one another. We knew that was the title.

Once we established it Whitley commented on what a great title it was. I pointed out to him it was he who gave us the title. He had forgotten. But in the end I felt it very appropriate that Whitley named our show.

For the next year we shot the pilot on weekends when people we were working with had the available time to give. Everyone that had contributed did so on deferment because they loved the project and wanted to see it succeed. We were blessed to have all the wonderful, talented people on our crew and the actors. Many are old friends from my years in the industry.

Here is the list of end credits to the show.

Lead Cast

Whitley Strieber	Whitley Strieber
Jeff Bond	Mark and Alien
Logan Bond	Mark
Robb Wolford	Grandfather and Robb
Tammy Klein	Grandmother
Peter Fox	Gardener
Steve Altman	Steve Altman

Supporting Cast

Julie Fox	Support Group
David Alan Graf	G-Man and Support Group
Yvonne Smith	Yvonne Smith
Giselle Arzola	Alien
Kim Roesenbrock	Mark's parent
Scott Mark	Mark's parent
April Malloy	Support Group
Brent Clark	Support Group
Tanya Owl Bear	Support Group

Director:

Steve Neill

Writer

Steve Neill

Producers

Paul Gentry, Whitley Strieber, John Catalano and
Isaac Blair

Executive Producers

Steve Neill and Mary Cacciapaglia

Director of Photography

Paul Gentry

Production Designer
Steve Neill

Editor

Isaac Blair

Costume Designer
Mary Cacciapaglia

Music Composer
Thomas Martin

First Assistant Director
Mary Cacciapaglia

Grip

John Catalano, Jr.

Electric

John Catalano

John Catalano, Jr.

Camera

John Catalano

Tim Ogglesbee

This gives you an idea of how many wonderful people supported us and gave of their talent. I can't thank them all enough. As I write this, we are in the final stages of editing and visual effects.

I have produced and written film before, however this time, it was all my idea and I had all the control. It has been an amazing experience, too. Directing actors and re-creating scenes from my life were unlike anything I ever experienced. As I sit in editorial daily and watch the show come together, sometimes I am moved to tears. They are tears of joy because I was finally able to do my story the way it happened; the way it happens for many.

If you have had this experience, you are not alone. You should never be afraid of the unknown, but rather to embrace it. We are born of the stars. How could anything be more wonderful and amazing than that?

Epilogue

It's been a long and difficult journey writing this book and making the TV pilot. It has also been amazing and wonderful.

Writing this book was difficult. It is difficult reviewing ones life going back 65 years. It is amazing and wonderful because I could remember most of it, as if it happened yesterday. It is fascinating to observe the growth of ones soul as it learns and explores reality. I could feel it, as if I relived it because it is my life. Past, present, and future are all just words. It is always now and everything exists in this now.

All through the book I have described how it feels to have a life surrounded in the mystery of the Visitor experience. It is a broad term for so many different experiences, but in the end I see that they are all deeply related; they are all one. When we lose our physical form, our souls, our spirits will often be returned to the Great Spirit much like a cup of water to the ocean. We lose all sense of self and are lost. This makes me think of that great scene in "Blade Runner" when the Replican says, as he's dying, "All those memories lost, like tears in rain". That resonated with me when I heard it the first time. If we are to ascend and retain the consistency of our souls, of our memories, and things we have loved and learned, then we need to work hard to achieve this. We need to raise our consciousness. As a species, we seem to live in a bubble, one that does not include the greater reality of our vast Cosmos. By comparison, our existence on Earth can be a small matter compared to the trillions of stars and lives that live and die in their universes. We tend to believe, not know, that the realm of the dead is separate from that of the living, when in my opinion, they are not. This experience has shown me this, time and time again. Nothing ever really dies. We are all connected to every living thing throughout the Cosmos and beyond that everyone we have ever known. It is said that is you shatter a hologram and examine the pieces, you will find that in every shroud of glass of that hologram is the entire hologram. You can take a hologram and break it in many pieces so small you can't see the whole image anymore until you look under magnification and there it still remains whole. We are all part of a whole; we are part of a force that connects us all. Our existence is huge, not small.

Star Wars had it right. Some call it God, some call it Allah, and many others have different names for it. But it's all the same spirit. But when we separate ourselves and isolate from the spirit, we become dysfunctional. This has created the state of affairs we are now experiencing on Earth. We make our own reality bubble, where all that remains is the Earth with its troubles, fears, wars and hate. Some don't even acknowledge the stars at night or acknowledge the one closest to us, our fantastic sun. The sun gave birth to all of us. Many believe we are separate from nature and that we don't have to follow her laws. Worst of all, we see ourselves as separate races instead of different cultures. We are one race, The Human Race. Beyond this small Earth lays a huge Universe full of wonder just beckoning us to explore it. We are already there if you just notice. We need to ascend and spread our wings to the stars with love. The message from the Visitors is quite simple. It's not complicated. Anne Strieber said it best, "Have Joy."

A friend, who was having the experience, told me how much fear he held, that he hated the Visitors and even wanted to kill them. He felt that this experience was destroying his life. I said to him, "But you're awake now, right?" He looked at me perplexed. "What did I mean?" I told him before he had these experiences that he was asleep. He was asleep in the dream made up of right and wrong, of absolutes and authority that was meant not to be questioned, a flat plain of existence which merely included birth, growing up, work and death. Now you're questioning that reality because you just learned that all you have been taught might not be true. There is more, much more. You have awakened from your sleep. A sleep where we were all placed. He had never thought of it that way before. It changed things for him and he started to view his experience differently.

Like the apes in 2001, the Visitors had awakened us. Just like in "2001, A Space Odyssey" we have touched the monolith. We are forever changing. They evolved and were set on a path of higher consciousness, as we are. Humans will, in the end, have an evolution of consciousness, a Communion with the Cosmos and a knowing of it. Remember the "Star Child" floating over Earth at the end of 2001? So many didn't understand the film. It is a simple message: one day, through our interaction with the spirit of this amazing universe, we will achieve higher consciousness.

Steve Neill is an artist, visual effects creator, and filmmaker with over 40 years of experience in film and television industry.

In 1971 he interned at the American Zoetrope in San Francisco with Francis Ford Coppola and received much of his film making education there. He moved to Hollywood to pursue his career in 1974.

Steve has since worked on movies such as "Star Trek the Motion Picture", "Ghost Busters", "Fright Night" and more. He has appeared as a creature suit actor in many films, commercials and TV shows. In addition he wrote and produced the feature film, "The Day Time Ended."

Steve owns SNG Studio, a film studio in Ventura California where he works with his partner, Mary Cacciapaglia producing visual effect, postproduction, model miniatures, creatures and prosthetic makeup.

He has had lifelong experiences with non-human intelligence starting when he was 6 years old. He first became aware of memories he thought were unique to him were also shared by others when he first read "Communion", by Whitley Strieber. He later in 1991 met and worked with Yvonne Smith to recover more of his memories of his lifelong encounters. This lead to a plethora of artwork, sculpture and visual effects work on the subject of encounters with non-humans that has since characterized the look of the grey alien beings we see today. He also during the 90s appeared on numerous talk shows, TV series and documentaries on the UFO subject. His work was seen worldwide and used on such shows as "Sightings", "Paranormal Borderline", the History Channels "UFO Files" and a multitude of documentaries.

Today Steve has created, written, and directed a new dramatic series about his experience. He tells his story without theories, conjecture and folklore. But rather an honest reporting of what he has experienced. The series is entitled, *"But Something is There"* because he doesn't know what this intelligence is, only that it is there.

Resource Information List

Whitley Strieber – Author www.strieber.com

Travis Walton – Author *Fire In The Sky* -
www.travis-walton.com

Dr. Roger Leir – *www.* alienjigsaw.com

CERO INTERNATIONAL (close Encounters Research Organization – Yvonne Smith, C.Ht. President –www.cerointernational.com

Arial Phenomena – www.aerial-phenomenon.org
API is a worldwide UFO investigations team about
the scientific investigation of unidentified aerial phenomena

Made in the USA
Middletown, DE
07 November 2020